ESSENTIAL KOREAN READING COMPREHENSION WORKBOOK :
Multi-Level Practice Sets With Over 500 Questions
ISBN 979-11-88195-52-7

Ordering Information: Quantity sales. Special discounts are available on quantity purchases by corporations, associations, and others. For details, contact the publisher at the email address above.

Printed in the United States of America

www.newampersand.com

14 13 12 11 10 / 10 9 8 7 6 5 4 3 2 1

Practice #1 (Difficulty ★☆☆☆☆)

Read the following passage carefully and answer the following questions.

제 이름은 선호입니다. [je i-reum-eun seon-ho-ip-ni-da.]

저는 학생입니다. [jeo-neun hak-saeng-ip-ni-da.]

저는 소년입니다. [jeo-neun so-nyeon-ip-ni-da.]

저는 부산에서 왔습니다. [jeo-neun bu-san-e-seo wa-sseup-ni-da.]

저는 열살입니다. [jeo-neun yeol-sal-ip-ni-da.]

저의 취미는 운동입니다. [jeo-eui chwi-mi-neun un-dong-ip-ni-da.]

저는 겨울을 가장 좋아합니다. [jeo-neun gyeo-ul-eul ga-jang jo-a-hap-ni-da.]

Question 1. According to the passage, 선호 is the (   ) of the speaker.

1. Hobby 2. Name 3. Age 4. Hometown 5. Occupation

Question 2. What does the speaker do? He/she is a...

1. Teacher 2. Soccer Player 3. Musician 4. Magician 5. Student

Question 3. According to the passage, the speaker is a...?

1. Boy 2. Girl 3. Senior Citizen 4. Baby 5. Twin

Question 4. According to the passage, 부산 is the speaker's...

1. Hobby 2. Name 3. Age 4. Hometown 5. Occupation

Question 5. How old is the speaker?

1. Five 2. Six 3. Ten 4. Eleven 5. Fifteen

Question 6. What does the speaker do for fun (= hobby)?

1. Study 2. Exercise 3. Play Video Games 4. Read 5. Sleep

Question 7. According to the passage, what is the speaker's favorite season?

1. Spring 2. Summer 3. Autumn 4. Winter

Practice #2 (Difficulty ★ ☆ ☆ ☆ ☆)

Read the following passage carefully and answer the following questions.

진수와 미나는 친구입니다. [jin-su-wa mi-na-neun chin-gu-ip-ni-da.]

진수의 집과 미나의 집은 가깝습니다. [jin-su-eui jib-gwa mi-na-eui jib-eun ga-kkap-seup-ni-da.]

진수와 미나는 같은 학교에 다닙니다. [jin-su-wa mi-na-neun ga-teun hak-gyo-e da-nip-ni-da.]

그들은 학교에서 같은 수업을 듣습니다. [geu-deul-eun hak-gyo-e-seo ga-teun su-eob-eul deut-sseup-ni-da.]

진수와 미나는 학교에서 점심을 같이 먹습니다.
[jin-su-wa mi-na-neun hak-gyo-e-seo jeom-shim-eul ga-chi meok-seup-ni-da.]

월요일과 수요일에는 학교에 같이 갑니다. [wol-yo-il-gwa su-yo-il-e-neun hak-gyo-e ga-chi gap-ni-da.]

일요일에는 교회에 함께 갑니다. [il-yo-il-e-neun gyo-hoe-e ham-kke gap-ni-da.]

Question 1. According to the passage, 진수 and 미나 are...?

1. Co-workers 2. Friends 3. Relatives 4. Sister and Brother 5. Enemies

Question 2. According to the passage, their homes are...?

1. Close To Each Other 2. Far From Each Other 3. Within Walking Distance 4. In Different Countries

Question 3. True or False? They go to different schools.

1. True 2. False

Question 4. True or False? They have the same classes at school.

1. True 2. False

Question 5. True or False? They have breakfast together at school.

1. True 2. False

Question 6. According to the passage, they do what together on Monday and Wednesday?

1. Go To School 2. Study 3. Pray 4. Have Breakfast

Question 7. According to the passage, what do they do together on Sunday?

1. Volunteer Work 2. Go To Church 3. Study English 4. Watch a Movie 5. Do Homework

Practice #3 (Difficulty ★ ☆ ☆ ☆ ☆)

Read the following passage carefully and answer the following questions.

오늘은 민수의 생일입니다. [o-neul-eun min-su-eui saeng-il-ip-ni-da.]

민수는 이제 열세살 입니다. [min-su-neun i-je yeol-se-sal ip-ni-da.]

친구들이 민수에게 선물을 주었습니다. [chin-gu-deul-i min-su-e-ge seon-mul-eul ju-eot-sseup-ni-da.]

민수가 가장 좋아한 선물은 축구공입니다. [min-su-ga ga-jang jo-a-han seon-mul-eun chuk-gu-gong-ip-ni-da.]

민수는 친구들과 저녁을 먹었습니다. [min-su-neun chin-gu-deul-gwa jeo-nyeok-eul meok-eot-sseup-ni-da.]

친구들이 민수를 위해 노래를 불렀습니다.
[chin-gu-deul-i min-su-reul-wi-hae no-rae-reul bul-leot-sseup-ni-da.]

민수는 행복했습니다. [min-su-neun haeng-bok-haet-sseup-ni-da.]

Question 1. According to the passage, today is 민수's...

1. Graduation 2. Birthday 3. Moving Day 4. Promotion Day 5. 1 Year Wedding Anniversary

Question 2. How old is 민수?

1. Five 2. Ten 3. Thirteen 4. Fifteen 5. Twenty

Question 3. According to the passage, who gave 민수 the birthday presents?

1. Relatives 2. Fans 3. Co-workers 4. Colleagues 5. Friends

Question 4. According to the passage, 민수's favorite present was...

1. Tennis Ball 2. Baseball Glove 3. Soccer Ball 4. Superman T-Shirt 5. Cake

Question 5. What did 민수 do with his friends?

1. Had Dinner 2. Watched a Movie 3. Played Soccer 4. Played Video Games 5. Went Hiking

Question 6. What did the friends do for 민수 ?

1. Sang a Song 2. Made a Video Clip 3. Made a Handmade Cookie 4. Took Photos 5. Cleaned House

Question 7. According to the passage, how did 민수 feel?

1. Upset 2. Confused 3. Excited 4. Happy 5. Hyper

Practice #4 (Difficulty ★ ☆ ☆ ☆ ☆)

Read the following passage carefully and answer the following questions.

토마스는 어학당에서 공부합니다. [to-ma-seu-neun eo-hak-dang-e-seo gong-bu-hap-ni-da.]

토마스의 전공은 한국어입니다. [to-ma-seu-eui jeon-gong-eun han-guk-eo-ip-ni-da.]

공부를 한지 육개월 되었습니다. [gong-bu-reul han-ji yuk-gae-wol doe-eot-sseup-ni-da.]

한국어는 문법이 어렵습니다. [han-guk-eo-neun mun-beop-i eo-ryeop-sseup-ni-da.]

하지만 한국인 친구들이 많이 도와줍니다. [ha-ji-man han-guk-in chin-gu-deul-i man-i do-wa-jup-ni-da.]

숙제가 많을때에는, 다른 외국인 친구들과 함께 공부합니다.
[suk-je-ga man-eul-ttae-e-neun, da-reun oe-guk-in chin-gu-deul-gwa ham-kke gong-bu-hap-ni-da.]

한국어를 배워서, 여행을 하고 싶습니다. [han-guk-eo-reul bae-wo-seo, yeo-haeng-eul ha-go ship-seup-ni-da.]

Question 1. According to the passage, where does 토마스 study?

1. Kindergarten 2. Culture Center 3. Language School 4. Church 5. Home

Question 2. According to the passage, 토마스's major is...

1. Russian 2. Korean 3. English 4. Japanese 5. Spanish

Question 3. How long has 토마스 been studying Korean?

1. Three Months 2. Five Months 3. Six Months 4. Two Years 5. Three Years

Question 4. According to the passage, what's difficult about Korean?

1. Pronunciation 2. Spelling 3. Reading 4. Writing 5. Grammar

Question 5. According to the passage, who helps 토마스 study?

1. Family 2. Foreign Friends 3. Korean Friends 4. Teacher 5. Counselor

Question 6. When there's a lot of homework, who does 토마스 study with?

1. Other Foreign Students 2. Korean Friends 3. Volunteers 4. Alone 5. Counselors

Question 7. According to the passage, what does 토마스 want to do with learning Korean?

1. Become a Translator 2. Write a Novel 3. Travel 4. Become an Entertainer 5. Become a Politician

Read the following passage carefully and answer the following questions.

오늘은 월요일입니다. [o-neul-eun wol-yo-il-ip-ni-da.]

아침 일찍 일어났습니다. [a-chim il-jjik il-eo-nat-sseup-ni-da.]

일곱시 삼십분에 일어났어요. [il-gop-shi sam-ship-bun-e il-eo-nat-sseo-yo.]

빵과 우유를 먹었습니다. [bbang-gwa u-yu-reul meok-eot-sseup-ni-da.]

지하철을 타고 회사에 갔습니다. [ji-ha-cheol-eul ta-go hoe-sa-e gat-sseup-ni-da.]

하지만, 회사에 아무도 없었습니다. [ha-ji-man, hoe-sa-e a-mu-do eo-eot-sseup-ni-da.]

공휴일이었기 때문입니다. [gong-hyu-il-i-eot-gi ttae-mun-ip-ni-da.]

Question 1. According to the passage, today is...

1. Sunday 2. Monday 3. Wednesday 4. Friday 5. Saturday

Question 2. Did the speaker wake up...

1. Early In The Morning 2. Late In The Morning 3. Same Time As Usual 4. Late In The Afternoon

Question 3. According to the passage, what time did the speaker wake up?

1. 5:30 2. 6:15 3. 7:30 4. 9:45 5. 11:30

Question 4. According to the passage, what did the speaker eat?

1. Bread and Rice 2. Rice and Kimchi 3. Fried Rice 4. Bread and Milk 5. Bagel and Coffee

Question 5. How did the speaker get to work?

1. Subway 2. Taxi 3. Walk 4. Bus 5. Car Pool

Question 6. When he got to work, who did the speaker find?

1. Boss 2. Manager 3. Security Guard 4. Co-worker 5. Nobody

Question 7. According to the passage, it happened because it was a...

1. Company Retreat Day 2. Public Holiday 3. Promotion Day 4. Temporary Holiday

Practice #6 (Difficulty ★ ☆ ☆ ☆ ☆)

Read the following passage carefully and answer the following questions.

세미는 여행을 할 예정입니다. [se-mi-neun da-eum-dal-e yeo-haeng-eul gap-ni-da.]

미국에 갈 것입니다. [mi-guk-e gal ye-jeong-ip-ni-da.]

친구들을 만나서 해변에 갈 것입니다. [chin-gu-deul-eul man-na-seo ba-da-e gal geo-ship-ni-da.]

마술 쇼도 볼 것입니다. [ma-sul sho-do bol geo-ship-ni-da.]

일주일 정도 있을 계획입니다. [il-ju-il jeong-do it-sseul gye-hoek-ip-ni-da.]

한국과 시차는 열 시간입니다. [han-guk-gwa shi-cha-neun yeol shi-gan-ip-ni-da.]

한국이 오후 한시면, 미국은 오전 세시 입니다.
[han-guk-i o-hu han-shi-myeon, mi-guk-eun o-jeon se-shi ip-ni-da.]

Question 1. According to the passage, what does 세미 plan on doing?

1. Study 2. Apply for College 3. Volunteer 4. Travel 5. Learn To Play Piano

Question 2. According to the passage, 세미 will be visiting...

1. Russia and Japan 2. China and Japan 3. USA 4. Mexico and France 5. Brazil

Question 3. Where will 세미 go with friends?

1. Shopping Mall 2. Beach 3. Mountain 4. National Park 5. Museum

Question 4. What will 세미 see/watch?

1. Magic Show 2. Opera 3. Movie 4. K-pop Concert 5. Circus

Question 5. How long does 세미 plan on staying there for?

1. About Three Days 2. About A Week 3. About Two Weeks 4. About A Month 5. About A Year

Question 6. According to the passage, what's the time difference?

1. Five Hours 2. Seven Hours 3. Ten Hours 4. Twelve Hours 5. Fourteen Hours

Question 7. According to the passage, when it's 1 PM in Korea, what time is it there?

1. Two AM 2. Three AM 3. Six AM 4. Nine PM 5. Eleven PM

Practice #7 (Difficulty ★ ☆ ☆ ☆ ☆)

Read the following passage carefully and answer the following questions.

오늘은 날씨가 좋지 않습니다. [o-neul-eun nal-ssi-ga jot-chi an-seup-ni-da.]

비가 많이 내리고 있어요. [bi-ga man-i nae-ri-go it-sseo-yo.]

바람은 많이 불지 않아요. [ba-ram-eun man-i bul-ji an-a-yo.]

하지만 날씨는 따뜻합니다. [ha-ji-man nal-ssi-neun tta-tteut-hap-ni-da.]

우산이 없는 사람은 건물에서 기다립니다. [u-san-i eop-neun sa-ram-eun geon-mul-e-seo gi-da-rip-ni-da.]

비는 곧 그칠 것 같습니다. [bi-neun got geu-chil geot gat-seup-ni-da.]

이번 주 내내 계속 비가 온다고 합니다. [i-beon ju nae-nae gye-sok bi-ga on-da-go hap-ni-da.]

Question 1. According to the passage, the weather today is...

1. Pleasant 2. Fickle 3. Predictable 4. Not Nice 5. Same As Usual

Question 2. True or False? It's snowing heavily.

1. True 2. False

Question 3. True or False? It's very windy.

1. True 2. False

Question 4. According to the passage, the temperature is...

1. Cold 2. Hot 3. Warm 4. Freezing 5. Perfect

Question 5. According to the passage, people who don't have an umbrella...

1. Stay Home 2. Wait Inside a Building 3. Take Bus 4. Share an Umbrella 5. Buy an Umbrella

Question 6. According to the passage, it seems like...

1. Rain Will Continue 2. Rain Will Turn Into Snow 3. Rain Will Stop Soon 4. More Rain Is Expected

Question 7. According to the passage, the weather for the rest of the week will be...

1. Sunny 2. Cloudy 3. Snowy 4. Dry 5. Rainy

Practice #8 (Difficulty ★ ☆ ☆ ☆ ☆)

Read the following passage carefully and answer the following questions.

저의 집은 대구에 있습니다. [jeo-eui jip-eun dae-gu-e it-seup-ni-da.]

서울에서 버스로 약 네시간 거리입니다. [seo-ul-e-seo bu-seu-ro yak ne-shi-gan geo-ri-ip-ni-da.]

기차를 타면 절반 정도 걸립니다. [gi-cha-reul ta-myeon jeol-ban jeong-do geol-lip-ni-da.]

대구는 정말 덥습니다. [dae-gu-neun jeong-mal deop-seup-ni-da.]

한국에서 가장 더운 곳 입니다. [han-guk-e-seo ga-jang deo-un got ip-ni-da.]

대구는 사과가 유명합니다. [dae-gu-neun sa-gwa-ga yu-myeong-hap-ni-da.]

대구 사과는 달고, 영양소가 많아 유명합니다.
[dae-gu sa-gwa-neun dal-go, yeong-yang-so-ga man-a yu-myeong-hap-ni-da.]

Question 1. According to the passage, the speaker's (   ) is in Daegu.

1. School 2. Hospital 3. Library 4. Home 5. Church

Question 2. According to the passage, how far is it from Seoul to Daegu, by bus?

1. One Hour 2. Two Hours 3. Three Hours 4. Four Hours 5. Five Hours

Question 3. According to the passage, taking the train will take how much more/less time?

1. Half 2. Double 3. 1/3 4. Triple 5. No Change

Question 4. According to the passage, the weather in Daegu is...

1. Cold 2. Hot 3. Warm 4. Fickle 5. Rainy

Question 5. True or False? Daegu is the hottest place in Korea.

1. True 2. False

Question 6. According to the passage, Daegu is famous for...

1. Orange 2. Banana 3. Pear 4. Strawberry 5. Apple

Question 7. According to the passage, Daegu apples are famous for having a rich amount of...

1. Mineral 2. Energy 3. Water 4. Nutrients 5. Calories

Practice #9 (Difficulty ★ ☆ ☆ ☆ ☆)

Read the following passage carefully and answer the following questions.

저의 취미는 음악 듣기 입니다. [jeo-eui chwi-mi-neun eum-ak deut-gi ip-ni-da.]

음악을 들으면 마음이 편해져서 좋습니다.
[eum-ak-eul deul-eu-myeon ma-eum-i pyeon-hae-jyeo-seo jot-seup-ni-da.]

하지만 너무 시끄러운 음악은 싫어합니다.
[ha-ji-man neo-mu shi-kkeu-reo-un eum-ak-eun shil-eo-hap-ni-da.]

친구들과 공연장에 가는 것 도 좋아합니다.
[chin-gu-deul-gwa gong-yeon-jang-e ga-neun geot do jo-a-hap-ni-da.]

지난 주에는 재즈 공연에 갔습니다. [ji-nan ju-e-neun jae-jeu gong-yeon-e gat-sseup-ni-da.]

관람객이 약 백 명 정도 있었습니다. [bi-neun got geu-chil geot gat-seup-ni-da.]

내년에도 다시 가고 싶습니다. [nae-nyeon-e-do da-shi ga-go ship-seup-ni-da.]

Question 1. According to the passage, the speaker's hobby is...?

1. Listening to Music 2. Watching a Movie 3. Hiking 4. Studying 5. Reading a Novel

Question 2. According to the passage, doing so makes him/her feel...

1. Excited 2. Elated 3. Comfortable 4. Smart 5. Joyful

Question 3. According to the passage, the speaker doesn't like THIS, though...

1. Scary Movie 2. Loud Music 3. Sad Novel 4. Dangerous Trails 5. Difficult Subject

Question 4. According to the passage, the speaker enjoys his/her hobby with...

1. Parents 2. Colleagues 3. Co-workers 4. Friends 5. Fan Club Members

Question 5. According to the passage, the speaker went to THIS last week...

1. K-Pop Concert 2. Outdoor Theater 3. Book Reading Club 4. Jazz Concert 5. Opera

Question 6. According to the passage, how many people (audience) were there?

1. About 50 2. About 100 3. About 150 4. About 1,000 5. Exactly 50

Question 7. True or False? The speaker wants to go to the event again next year.

1. True 2. False

Practice #10 (Difficulty ★ ☆ ☆ ☆ ☆)

Read the following passage carefully and answer the following questions.

저의 가족은 다섯 명 입니다. [jeo-eui ga-jok-eun da-seot myeong ip-ni-da.]

엄마, 아빠, 누나, 여동생, 남동생이 있습니다 .
[eom-ma, appa, nu-na, yeo-dong-saeng, nam-dong-saeng-i it-sseup-ni-da.]

엄마는 선생님입니다. [eom-ma-neun seon-saeng-nim-ip-ni-da.]

누나와 저는 세 살 차이입니다. [nu-na-wa jeo-neun se sal cha-i-ip-ni-da.]

여동생과 남동생은 사이가 좋습니다. [yeo-dong-saeng-gwa nam-dong-saeng-eun sa-i-ga jot-seup-ni-da.]

저희는 매주 일요일, 함께 교회에 갑니다. [jeo-hi-neun mae-ju il-yo-il, ham-kke gyo-hwe-e gap-ni-da.]

교회가 끝나면, 맛있는 저녁을 먹고 집에 돌아옵니다.
[gyo-hwe-ga kkeut-na-myeon, ma-shit-neun jeo-nyeok-eul meok-go jip-e dol-a-op-ni-da.]

Question 1. According to the passage, the speaker's family has how many members?

1. Three 2. Four 3. Five 4. Six 7. Seven

Question 2. According to the passage, which of the following is NOT in the family?

1. Mother 2. Father 3. Grand Mother 4. Younger Sister 5. Older Sister

Question 3. According to the passage, what does the speaker's mother do?

1. Student 2. Teacher 3. Principal 4. Counselor 5. House Wife

Question 4. According to the passage, the older sister and the speaker are how many years apart?

1. Two 2. Three 3. Four 4. Five 5. Six

Question 5. True or False? The younger sister and the younger brother get along with each other.

1. True 2. False

Question 6. According to the passage, the family goes HERE every Sunday.

1. Movie Theater 2. Beach 3. Church 4. Library 5. Opera House

Question 7. According to the passage, what do they do before coming back home?

1. Eat Ice Cream 2. Go Shopping 3. Have Delicious Dinner 4. Visit Relatives 5. Take a Photo

Practice #1

제 이름은 선호입니다. My name is Seon-ho.
[je i-reum-eun seon-ho-ip-ni-da.]
저는 학생입니다. I am a student.
[jeo-neun hak-saeng-ip-ni-da.]
저는 소년입니다. I am a boy.
[jeo-neun so-nyeon-ip-ni-da.]
저는 부산에서 왔습니다. I am from Busan.
[jeo-neun busan-e-seo wat-seup-ni-da.]
저는 열살입니다. I am ten years old.
[jeo-neun yeol-sal-ip-ni-da.]
저의 취미는 운동입니다. My hobby is exercising.
[jeo-eui chwi-mi-neun un-dong-ip-ni-da.]
저는 겨울을 가장 좋아합니다. I like winter the most.
[jeo-neun gyeo-ul-eul ga-jang jo-a-hap-ni-da.]

Answer Keys : (1) **2** (2) **5** (3) **1** (4) **4** (5) **3** (6) **2** (7) **4**

Practice #2

진수와 미나는 친구입니다. Jinsu and Mina are friends.
[jin-su-wa mi-na-neun chin-gu-ip-ni-da.]
진수의 집과 미나의 집은 가깝습니다. Jinsu and Mina's homes are close to each other.
[jin-su-eui jib-gwa mi-na-eui jib-eun ga-kkap-seup-ni-da.]
진수와 미나는 같은 학교에 다닙니다. Jinsu and Mina go to same school.
[jin-su-wa mi-na-neun ga-teun hak-gyo-e da-nip-ni-da.]
그들은 학교에서 같은 수업을 듣습니다. They take the same class(es) at school.
[geu-deul-eun hak-gyo-e-seo ga-teun su-eob-eul deut-sseup-ni-da.]
진수와 미나는 학교에서 점심을 같이 먹습니다. Jinsu and Mina eat lunch together at school.
[jin-su-wa mi-na-neun hak-gyo-e-seo jeom-shim-eul ga-chi meok-seup-ni-da.]
월요일과 수요일에는 학교에 같이 갑니다. (They) go to school together on Monday and Wednesday.
[wol-yo-il-gwa su-yo-il-e-neun hak-gyo-e ga-chi gap-ni-da.]
일요일에는 교회에 함께 갑니다. (They) go to church together on Sunday.
[il-yo-il-e-neun gyo-hoe-e ham-kke gap-ni-da.]

Answer Keys : (1) 2 (2) 1 (3) 2 (4) 1 (5) 2 (6) 1 (7) 2

Practice #3

오늘은 민수의 생일입니다. Today is Minsu's birthday.
[o-neul-eun min-su-eui saeng-il-ip-ni-da.]
민수는 이제 열세살 입니다. Minsu is thirteen-years-old now.
[min-su-neun i-je yeol-se-sal ip-ni-da.]
친구들이 민수에게 선물을 주었습니다. Friends gave Minsu gifts.
[chin-gu-deul-i min-su-e-ge seon-mul-eul ju-eot-sseup-ni-da.]
민수가 가장 좋아한 선물은 축구공입니다. The gift Minsu liked the most was a soccer ball.
[min-su-ga ga-jang jo-a-han seon-mul-eun chuk-gu-gong-ip-ni-da.]
민수는 친구들과 저녁을 먹었습니다. Minsu had dinner with friends.
[min-su-neun chin-gu-deul-gwa jeo-nyeok-eul meok-eot-sseup-ni-da.]
친구들이 민수를 위해 노래를 불렀습니다. Friends sang a song for Minsu.
[chin-gu-deul-i min-su-reul-wi-hae no-rae-reul bul-leot-sseup-ni-da.]
민수는 행복했습니다. Minsu was happy.
[min-su-neun haeng-bok-haet-sseup-ni-da.]

Answer Keys : (1) 2 (2) 3 (3) 5 (4) 3 (5) 1 (6) 1 (7) 4

Practice #4

토마스는 어학당에서 공부합니다. Thomas is studying at a language school.
[to-ma-seu-neun eo-hak-dang-e-seo gong-bu-hap-ni-da.]
토마스의 전공은 한국어입니다. Thomas' major is Korean.
[to-ma-seu-eui jeon-gong-eun han-guk-eo-ip-ni-da.]
공부를 한지 육개월 되었습니다. It's been six months since he's started studying.
[gong-bu-reul han-ji yuk-gae-wol doe-eot-sseup-ni-da.]
한국어는 문법이 어렵습니다. The grammar of Korean is difficult.
[han-guk-eo-neun mun-beop-i eo-ryeop-sseup-ni-da.]
하지만 한국인 친구들이 많이 도와줍니다. But Korean friends help (him) a lot.
[ha-ji-man han-guk-in chin-gu-deul-i man-i do-wa-jup-ni-da.]
숙제가 많을때에는, 다른 외국인 친구들과 함께 공부합니다.
When there's a lot of homework, (he) studies with other foreign friends.
[suk-je-ga man-eul-ttae-e-neun, da-reun oe-guk-in chin-gu-deul-gwa ham-kke gong-bu-hap-ni-da.]
한국어를 배워서, 여행을 하고 싶습니다.
(He) wants to learn Korean and travel.
[han-guk-eo-reul bae-wo-seo, yeo-haeng-eul ha-go ship-seup-ni-da.]

Answer Keys : (1) 3 (2) 2 (3) 3 (4) 5 (5) 3 (6) 1 (7) 3

Practice #5

오늘은 월요일입니다. Today is Monday.
[o-neul-eun wol-yo-il-ip-ni-da.]
아침 일찍 일어났습니다. I woke up early in the morning.
[a-chim il-jjik il-eo-nat-sseup-ni-da.]
일곱시 삼십분에 일어났어요. I woke up at seven-thirty.
[il-gop-shi sam-ship-bun-e il-eo-nat-sseo-yo.]
빵과 우유를 먹었습니다. I ate bread and milk.
[bbang-gwa u-yu-reul meok-eot-sseup-ni-da.]
지하철을 타고 회사에 갔습니다. I took the subway to work.
[ji-ha-cheol-eul ta-go hoe-sa-e gat-sseup-ni-da.]
하지만, 회사에 아무도 없었습니다. But there was no one at work.
[ha-ji-man, hoe-sa-e a-mu-do eo-eot-sseup-ni-da.]
공휴일이었기 때문입니다. It's because it was a holiday.
[gong-hyu-il-i-eot-gi ttae-mun-ip-ni-da.]

Answer Keys : (1) 2 (2) 1 (3) 3 (4) 4 (5) 1 (6) 5 (7) 2

Practice #6

세미는 여행을 할 예정입니다. Semi has a plan to travel.
[se-mi-neun da-eum-dal-e yeo-haeng-eul gap-ni-da.]
미국에 갈 것입니다. She is going to the U.S.A.
[mi-guk-e gal ye-jeong-ip-ni-da.]
친구들을 만나서 해변에 갈 것입니다. She will meet up with her friends and go to the beach.
[chin-gu-deul-eul man-na-seo ba-da-e gal geo-ship-ni-da.]
마술 쇼도 볼 것입니다. She will also watch a magic show.
[ma-sul sho-do bol geo-ship-ni-da.]
일주일 정도 있을 계획입니다. She plans to stay there for about a week.
[il-ju-il jeong-do it-sseul gye-hoek-ip-ni-da.]
한국과 시차는 열 시간입니다. The time difference with (= between) Korea (and the U.S.A) is ten hours.
[han-guk-gwa shi-cha-neun yeol shi-gan-ip-ni-da.]
한국이 오후 한시면, 미국은 오전 세시 입니다. If it's one in the afternoon, it's three in the morning in the U.S.A.
[han-guk-i o-hu han-shi-myeon, mi-guk-eun o-jeon se-shi ip-ni-da.]

Answer Keys : (1) 4 (2) 3 (3) 2 (4) 1 (5) 2 (6) 3 (7) 2

Practice #7

오늘은 날씨가 좋지 않습니다. The weather today is not good.
[o-neul-eun nal-ssi-ga jot-chi an-seup-ni-da.]
비가 많이 내리고 있어요. It's raining a lot.
[bi-ga man-i nae-ri-go it-sseo-yo.]
바람은 많이 불지 않아요. It's not very windy.
[ba-ram-eun man-i bul-ji an-a-yo.]
하지만 날씨는 따뜻합니다. But the weather is warm.
[ha-ji-man nal-ssi-neun tta-tteut-hap-ni-da.]
우산이 없는 사람은 건물에서 기다립니다. People without umbrellas are waiting inside a building.
[u-san-i eop-neun sa-ram-eun geon-mul-e-seo gi-da-rip-ni-da.]
비는 곧 그칠 것 같습니다. It seems to stop raining.
[bi-neun got geu-chil geot gat-seup-ni-da.]
이번 주 내내 계속 비가 온다고 합니다. It's said that it will be raining all week long.
[i-beon ju nae-nae gye-sok bi-ga on-da-go hap-ni-da.]

Answer Keys : (1) 4 (2) 2 (3) 2 (4) 3 (5) 2 (6) 3 (7) 5

Practice #8

저의 집은 대구에 있습니다. My home is in Daegu.
[jeo-eui jip-eun dae-gu-e it-seup-ni-da.]

서울에서 버스로 약 네시간 거리입니다. It's about four hours from Seoul by bus.
[seo-ul-e-seo bu-seu-ro yak ne-shi-gan geo-ri-ip-ni-da.]
기차를 타면 절반 정도 걸립니다. It takes about half the time if you take the train.
[gi-cha-reul ta-myeon jeol-ban jeong-do geol-lip-ni-da.]
대구는 정말 덥습니다. Daegu is really hot.
[dae-gu-neun jeong-mal deop-seup-ni-da.]
한국에서 가장 더운 곳 입니다. It's the hottest place in Korea.
[han-guk-e-seo ga-jang deo-un got ip-ni-da.]
대구는 사과가 유명합니다. Daegu is famous for apples.
[dae-gu-neun sa-gwa-ga yu-myeong-hap-ni-da.]
대구 사과는 달고, 영양소가 많아 유명합니다. Daegu apples are famous for being sweet and rich in nutritions.
[dae-gu sa-gwa-neun dal-go, yeong-yang-so-ga man-a yu-myeong-hap-ni-da.]

Answer Keys : (1) 4   (2) 4   (3) 1   (4) 2   (5) 1   (6) 5   (7) 4

Practice #9

저의 취미는 음악 듣기 입니다. My hobby is listening to music.
[jeo-eui chwi-mi-neun eum-ak deut-gi ip-ni-da.]
음악을 들으면 마음이 편해져서 좋습니다. I like it because listening to music makes me comfortable.
[eum-ak-eul deul-eu-myeon ma-eum-i pyeon-hae-jyeo-seo jot-seup-ni-da.]
하지만 너무 시끄러운 음악은 싫어합니다. But I dislike music that's too loud.
[ha-ji-man neo-mu shi-kkeu-reo-un eum-ak-eun shil-eo-hap-ni-da.]
친구들과 공연장에 가는 것 도 좋아합니다. I like going to concerts with friends, too.
[chin-gu-deul-gwa gong-yeon-jang-e ga-neun geot do jo-a-hap-ni-da.]
지난 주에는 재즈 공연에 갔습니다. I went to a jazz concert last week.
[ji-nan ju-e-neun jae-jeu gong-yeon-e gat-sseup-ni-da.]
관람객이 약 백 명 정도 있었습니다. There were about a hundred people in the audience.
[bi-neun got geu-chil geot gat-seup-ni-da.]
내년에도 다시 가고 싶습니다. I'd like to go again next week.
[nae-nyeon-e-do da-shi ga-go ship-seup-ni-da.]

Answer Keys : (1) 1   (2) 3   (3) 2   (4) 4   (5) 4   (6) 2   (7) 1

Practice #10

저의 가족은 다섯 명 입니다. My family has five people.
[jeo-eui ga-jok-eun da-seot myeong ip-ni-da.]
엄마, 아빠, 누나, 여동생, 남동생이 있습니다. There are mom, dad, older sister, younger sister, and younger brother.
[eom-ma, appa, nu-na, yeo-dong-saeng, nam-dong-saeng-i it-sseup-ni-da.]
엄마는 선생님입니다. Mother is a teacher.
[eom-ma-neun seon-saeng-nim-ip-ni-da.]
누나와 저는 세 살 차이입니다. Older sister and I are three years apart.
[nu-na-wa jeo-neun se sal cha-i-ip-ni-da.]
여동생과 남동생은 사이가 좋습니다. Younger sister and younger borther get along well.
[yeo-dong-saeng-gwa nam-dong-saeng-eun sa-i-ga jot-seup-ni-da.]
저희는 매주 일요일, 함께 교회에 갑니다. We go to church together on Sunday every week.
[jeo-hi-neun mae-ju il-yo-il, ham-kke gyo-hwe-e gap-ni-da.]
교회가 끝나면, 맛있는 저녁을 먹고 집에 돌아옵니다. When church is over, we have a delicious dinner and come back home.
[gyo-hwe-ga kkeut-na-myeon, ma-shit-neun jeo-nyeok-eul meok-go jip-e dol-a-op-ni-da.]

Answer Keys : (1) 3   (2) 3   (3) 2   (4) 2   (5) 1   (6) 3   (7) 3

Read the following passage carefully and answer the following questions.

저는 다음 달에 한국에 갑니다.
[jeo-neun da-eum dal-e han-guk-e gap-ni-da.]

한국에는 세 번 가 본 적이 있습니다.
[han-guk-e-neun se beon ga bon jeok-i it-seup-ni-da.]

여름에 두 번, 겨울에 한 번 가봤습니다.
[yeo-reum-e du-beon, gyeo-ul-e han beon ga-bwat-seup-ni-da.]

저는 겨울보다는 여름에 가는 것이 좋았습니다.
[jeo-neun gyeo-ul-bo-da-neun yeo-reum-e ga-neun geo-shi so-at-seup-ni-da.]

겨울에는 날씨가 추워서 밖에 나가기가 힘들었습니다.
[gyeo-ul-e-neun nal-ssi-ga chu-wo-seo bak-e na-ga-gi-ga him-deul-eot-seup-ni-da.]

제가 살고 있는 곳 보다 많이 춥습니다.
[je-ga sal-go it-neun dok-il-bo-da man-i chup-seup-ni-da.]

제가 가장 좋아한 곳은 박물관 입니다.
[je-ga ga-jang jo-a-han go-seun bak-mul-gwan ip-ni-da.]

한국의 미술에 관심이 많기 때문입니다.
[han-guk-eui mi-sul-e gwan-shim-i man-ki ttae-mun-ip-ni-da.]

한국의 불교 미술은 정말 아름답습니다.
[han-guk-eui bul-gyo mi-sul-eun jeong-mal a-reum-dap-seup-ni-da.]

그래서, 한국 미술을 공부할 계획입니다.
[geu-rae-seo, han-guk mi-sul-eul gong-bu-hal gye-hoek-ip-ni-da.]

한국의 미술을 독일 친구들에게 알리고 싶습니다.
[han-guk-eui mi-sul-eul dok-il chin-gu-deul-e-ge al-li-go ship-seup-ni-da.]

공부를 많이 해서, 한국 미술 전문가가 되고 싶습니다.
[gong-bu-reul man-i hae-seo, han-guk mi-sul jeon-mun-ga-ga doe-go ship-seup-ni-da.]

Question 1. According to the passage, when is the speaker's going to Korea?

1. Tomorrow 2. Next Week 3. Next Month 4. Next Year 5. Next Time

Question 2. According to the passage, how many times has the speaker been to Korea?

1. Once 2. Twice 3. Three Times 4. Four Times 5. Five Times

Question 3. True or False...? The speaker has been to Korea twice during the winter.

1. True 2. False

Question 4. True or False...? The speaker liked Korea's summer better than winter.

1. True 2. False

Question 5. True or False...? The speaker enjoyed the outdoor in Korea during the winter.

1. True 2. False

Question 6. According to the passage, how was Korea's weather compared to the speaker's home?

1. About the Same. 2. A Lot Colder in Korea 3. Little Colder Back Home 4. Hotter in Korea

Question 7. According to the passage, the speaker liked visiting WHERE the most?

1. Museum 2. Cafe 3. Concert 4. Folk Village 5. Gallery

Question 8. According to the passage, what is the speaker interested in?

1. Korean History 2. Korean Art 3. Korean Technology 4. Korean Movie 5. Korean Music

Question 9. According to the passage, the speaker thinks WHAT is beautiful?

1. Korean Houses 2. Korean Folk Art 3. Korean Royal Art 4. Korean Buddhist Art 5. Korean Pattern

Question 10. According to the passage, what does the speaker plan on doing?

1. Study Korean Art 2. Paint Korean Art 3. Purchase Korean Paintings 4. Learn the Korean Language

Question 11. According to the passage, what does the speaker wish to do?

1. Promote Korean Art 2. Learn Korean Culture 3. Write a Book On Korea History 4. Make Korean Friends

Question 12. According to the passage, the speaker wants to become...

1. A Buddhist 2. An Ambassador to Korea 3. A Teacher in Korea 4. A Korean Art Expert 5. A Linguist

Read the following passage carefully and answer the following questions.

한국에는 맛있는 음식이 많습니다.
[han-guk-e-neun ma-shit-neun eum-shik-i man-seup-ni-da.]

저는 아직 많은 한국 음식을 먹어보지 못했습니다.
[jeo-neun a-jik man-eun han-guk eum-shik-eul.meok-eo-bo-ji mot-haet-seup-ni-da.]

하지만 먹어본 것 중에서는 비빔밥을 좋아합니다.
[ha-ji-man meok-eo-bon geot jung-e-seo-neun bi-bim-bap-eul jo-a-hap-ni-da.]

다양한 재료가 들어있어, 영양소가 많습니다.
[da-yang-han jae-ryo-ga deul-eo-it-sseo, yeong-yang-so-ga man-seup-ni-da.]

비빔밥은 한국의 전통 음식입니다.
[bi-bim-bap-eun han-guk-eui jeon-tong eum-shik-ip-ni-da.]

왕과 일반인 모두 먹을 수 있었습니다.
[wang-gwa il-ban-in mo-du meok-eul su it-sseot-seup-ni-da.]

이제 비빔밥은 세계적인 음식이 되었습니다.
[i-je bi-bim-bap-eum se-gye-jeok-in eum-shik-i doe-eot-sseup-ni-da.]

외국인들도 비빔밥을 즐깁니다.
[oe-guk-in-deul-do bi-bim-bap-eul jeul-gip-ni-da.]

외국인들은 고추장을 넣지 않고 먹기도 합니다.
[oe-guk-in-deul-eun go-chu-jang-eul neot-ji an-go meok-gi-do hap-ni-da.]

외국인들에게는 너무 맵기 때문입니다.
[oe-guk-in-deul-e-ge-neun neo-mu maep-gi ttae-mun-ip-ni-da.]

하지만 저는 고추장을 많이 넣어 먹습니다.
[ha-ji-man jeo-neun go-chu-jang-eul man-i neo-eo meok-seup-ni-da.]

저는 매운 한국 음식을 좋아하기 때문입니다.
[jeo-neun mae-un han-guk eum-shik-eul jo-a-ha-gi ttae-mun-ip-ni-da.]

Question 1. According to the speaker, there are a lot of THIS in Korea.

1. Tasty Food 2. Fun Performances 3. Beautiful Mountains 4. Amazing Palaces 5. Good Looking People

Question 2. True or False...? The speaker tried almost every Korean food.

1. True 2. False

Question 3. True or False...? The speaker likes Bibimbap the most.

1. True 2. False

Question 4. According to the speaker, Bibimbap contains a lot of...

1. Nutrients 2. Calories 3. Minerals 4. Probiotics 5. Fiber

Question 5. True or False...? Bibimbap is a traditional Asian food.

1. True 2. False

Question 6. True or False...? Bibimbap could only be enjoyed by the King.

1. True 2. False

Question 7. According to the passage, Bibimbap is now what kind of food?

1. Global Food 2. Famous Food 3. Nutritious Food 4. Less Spicy Food 5. Spiciest Food

Question 8. True or False...? Foreigners enjoy Bibimbap too.

1. True 2. False

Question 9. According to the passage, some foreigners don't put THIS in Bibimbap.

1. Soy Sauce 2. Mayo 3. Sugar 4. Gochujang 5. Egg White

Question 10. According to the passage, they do that because it's too...

1. Salty 2. Hot (Spicy) 3. Weird 4. Sweet 5. Watery

Question 11. True or False...? The speaker puts a lot of Gochujang in Bibimbap.

1. True 2. False

Question 12. True or False...? The speaker likes spicy Korean food.

1. True 2. False

Read the following passage carefully and answer the following questions.

수요일과 금요일은 한국어 공부를 하는 날 입니다.
[su-yo-il-gwa geum-yo-il-eun han-guk-eo gong-bu-reul ha-neun nal ip-ni-da]

저희 한국어 선생님은 나이가 많으십니다.
[jeo-hui han-guk-eo seon-saeng-nim-eun na-i-ga man-eu-ship-ni-da.]

따라서, 경험이 많으십니다.
[tta-ra-seo, gyeong-heom-i man-eu-ship-ni-da.]

수업시간에는 매일 한국어 속담을 가르쳐 주십니다.
[su-eop-shi-gan-e-neun mae-il han-guk-eo sok-dam-eul ga-reu-chyeo ju-ship-ni-da.]

한국의 역사와 문화에 대해 많이 아십니다.
[han-guk-ui yeok-sa-wa mun-hwa-e dae-hae man-i a-ship-ni-da.]

수업시간은 다양한 국적의 학생들이 있습니다.
[su-eop-shi-gan-eun da-yang-han guk-jeok-ui hak-saeng-deul-i it-seup-ni-da.]

미국 학생이 가장 많고, 독일 학생은 한 명입니다.
[mi-guk hak-saeng-i ga-jang man-ko, dok-il hak-saeng-eun han myeong-ip-ni-da.]

아침 열 시 부터 오후 두 시 까지 수업입니다.
[a-chim yeol shi bu-teo o-hu du shi kka-ji su-eop-ip-ni-da.]

점심에는 모두 같이 모여서 식사를 합니다.
[jeom-shim-e-neum mo-du ga-chi mo-yeo-seo shik-sa-reul hap-ni-da.]

주로 한국 연예인 이야기를 많이 합니다.
[ju-ro han-guk yeon-ye-in i-ya-gi-reul man-i hap-ni-da.]

앞으로 약 육개월 정도 수업을 더 들어야 합니다.
[ap-eu-ro yak yuk-gae-wol jeong-do su-eop-eul deo deul-eo-ya hap-ni-da.]

수업을 다 듣고, 친구들과 함께 제주도로 여행을 갈 예정입니다.
[su-eop-eul da deut-go, chin-gu-deul-gwa ham-kke je-ju-do-ro yeo-haeng-eul gal ye-jeong-ip-ni-da.]

Question 1. According to the passage, when does the speaker study Korean?

1. Monday and Tuesday 2. Tuesday 3. Wednesday and Thursday 4. Thursday 5. Wednesday and Friday

Question 2. True or False...? The Korean language teacher is very young.

1. True 2. False

Question 3. According to the passage, the Korean language teacher is...

1. Strict 2. Professional 3. Scary 4. Smart 5. Highly Experienced

Question 4. According to the passage, the teacher teaches the students THIS every day.

1. Korean Slang Expressions 2. Korean Proverbs 3. Korean Music 4. Korean History 5. Korean Recipe

Question 5. According to the passage, the teacher knows a great deal about Korean...

1. Drama and Movie 2. Literature and Music 3. History and Culture 4. Traditional Dance and Games

Question 6. According to the passage, the class is composed of students of different...

1. Names 2. Nationalities 3. Cultures 4. Colors 5. Hometowns

Question 7. True or False...? There are more students from the US than from Germany.

1. True 2. False

Question 8. According to the passage, what time is the class?

1. 10 AM - 12 PM 2. 10 AM - 1 PM 3. 10 AM - 2 PM 4. 11 AM - 1 PM 5. 12 PM - 3 PM

Question 9. True or False...? Students go back to their dorm and have lunch separately.

1. True 2. False

Question 10. According to the passage, they mostly talk about THIS during lunch time.

1. Korean Entertainers 2. Korean Drama 3. Korean Writers 4. Korean Politicians 5. Korean Teachers

Question 11. According to the passage, how much longer would the class last?

1. Three Months 2. Four Months 3. Five Months 4. Six Months 5. Seven Months

Question 12. According to the passage, the students plan on doing THIS after class is finished.

1. Go On a Trip 2. Watch a Movie 3. Drink Soju 4. Record a K-Pop Cover Song 5. Volunteer

Read the following passage carefully and answer the following questions.

오늘은 눈이 많이 내린 하루였습니다.
[o-neul-eun nun-i man-i nae-rin ha-ru-yeot-seup-ni-da.]

오전부터 계속해서 내렸습니다.
[o-jeon-bu-teo gye-sok-hae-seo nae-ryeot-seup-ni-da.]

저녁이 되어서야 멈췄습니다.
[jeo-nyeok-i doe-eo-seo-ya meom-chwot-seup-ni-da.]

오전보다 오후에 눈이 더 많이 내렸습니다.
[o-jeon-bo-da o-hu-e nun-i deo-man-i nae-ryeot-seup-ni-da.]

많은 사람들이 길에서 넘어졌습니다.
[man-eun sa-ram-deul-i gil-e-seo neom-eo-jyeot-seup-ni-da.]

평소보다 지하철을 이용하는 사람들이 많았습니다.
[pyeong-so-bo-da ji-ha-cheol-eul i-yong-ha-neun sa-ram-deul-i man-at-seup-ni-da.]

다행히도, 눈이 쌓이지는 않았습니다.
[da-haeng-hi-do, nun-i ssa-i-ji-neun an-at-seup-ni-da.]

내일은 날씨가 따뜻할 것이라고 합니다.
[nae-il-eun nal-ssi-ga tta-tteut-hal geo-shi-ra-go hap-ni-da.]

집에서 나오기 전에, 항상 날씨를 확인해야합니다.
[jib-e-seo na-o-gi jeon-e, hang-sang nal-ssi-reul hwak-in-hae-ya-hap-ni-da.]

그리고, 작은 우산을 들고 다녀야합니다.
[geu-ri-go, jak-eun u-san-eul deul-go da-nyeo-ya-hap-ni-da.]

온도의 차이가 심해서, 감기에 걸리기 쉽습니다.
[on-do-eui cha-i-ga shim-hae-seo, gam-gi-e geol-li-gi ship-seup-ni-da.]

감기에 걸리면, 곧바로 병원에 가야합니다.
[gam-gi-e geol-li-myeon, got-ba-ro byeong-won-e ga-ya-hap-ni-da.]

Question 1. According to the passage, how was the weather?

1. Sunny 2. Windy 3. Rainy 4. Snowy 5. Freezing

Question 2. According to the passage, the weather condition mentioned above started...

1. In The Morning 2. During Lunch Time 3. In The Evening 4. In The Afternoon 5. After Dinner

Question 3. True or False...? It stopped just before lunch time.

1. True 2. False

Question 4. According to the passage, there was more of it in the morning than the afternoon.

1. True 2. False

Question 5. According to the passage, what happened to many people on the street?

1. They Fell 2. They Ran 3. They Walked Slowly 4. They Panicked 5. They Screamed

Question 6. True or False...? There were more people taking the subway than usual.

1. True 2. False

Question 7. According to the passage, how much of it got accumulated?

1. A Little Bit 2. Above Average 3. More Than Expected 4. Less Than Expected 5. Not At All

Question 8. According to the passage, tomorrow's weather is said to be...

1. Warm 2. Cold 3. Warm and Wet 4. Sunny and Windy 5. Mild and Calm

Question 9. According to the passage, what does the speaker say you have to do before leaving home?

1. Bring a Newspaper 2. Check The Weather 3. Close The Window 4. Lock The Door 5. Wash Hands

Question 10. According to the passage, what should you be carrying along witn you?

1. Wallet 2. Small Umbrella 3. Raincoat 4. Rainboots 5. Hat

Question 11. True or False...? It's easy to catch a cold because people stay inside.

1. True 2. False

Question 12. According to the passage, what should you do immediately when you catch a cold?

1. See A Doctor 2. Quarantine Yourself 3. Take Cold Medicine 4. Go To The Hospital 5. Stay Home

Read the following passage carefully and answer the following questions.

저의 꿈은 화가가 되는 것입니다.
[jeo-eui kkum-eun hwa-ga-ga doe-neun geo-ship-ni-da.]

어려서부터 그림을 그리는 것을 좋아했습니다.
[eo-ryeo-seo-bu-teo geu-ri-neun geo-seul jo-a-haet-seup-ni-da.]

많은 색 중에서 저는 분홍색을 가장 좋아합니다.
[man-eun saek jung-e-seo jeo-neun bun-hong-saek-eul ga-jang jo-a-hap-ni-da.]

분홍색을 보면 기분이 좋아집니다.
[bun-hong-saek-eul bo-myeon gi-bun-i jo-a-jip-ni-da.]

그래서 분홍색의 옷을 좋아합니다.
[geu-rae-seo bun-hong-saek-eui o-seul jo-a-hap-ni-da.]

그림을 그릴때에는 집중을 해야합니다.
[geu-rim-eul geu-ril-ttae-e-neun jip-jung-eul hae-ya-hap-ni-da.]

그래서 조용한 방에서 그림을 그립니다.
[geu-rae-seo jo-yong-han bang-e-seo geu-rim-eul geu-rip-ni-da.]

모두 잠이 든 새벽이 가장 조용합니다.
[mo-du jam-i deun sae-byeok-i ga-jang jo-yong-hap-ni-da.]

아름다운 그림을 그려서, 친구들에게 선물합니다.
[a-reum-da-un geu-rim-eul geu-ryeo-seo, chin-gu-deul-e-ge seon-mul-hap-ni-da.]

이번에는 귀여운 토끼를 그릴 계획입니다.
[i-beon-e-neun gwi-yeo-un to-kki-reul geu-ril-gye-hoek-ip-ni-da.]

동물을 그리는 것은 식물을 그리는 것 보다 어렵습니다.
[dong-mul-eul geu-ri-neun geo-seun shik-mul-eul geu-ri-neun geot bo-da eo-ryeop-seup-ni-da.]

계속해서 움직이기 때문입니다.
[gye-sok-hae-seo um-jik-i-gi tae-mun-ip-ni-da.]

Question 1. According to the passage, what's the speaker dreaming of becoming?

1. A Painter 2. A Musician 3. A Magician 4. A Teacher 5. An Athlete

Question 2. According to the passage, the speaker has been enjoying doing it since...

1. Little 2. Elementary School 3. Middle School 4. After Elementary School 5. After Highschool

Question 3. According to the passage, the speaker's favorite color is...?

1. Red 2. Blue 3. Yellow 4. Green 5. Pink

Question 4. According to the passage, the said color makes the speaker...

1. Feel Good 2. Focus 3. Become Creative 4. Calm Down 5. Get Excited

Question 5. According to the passage, the speaker likes WHAT of the said color?

1. Clothes 2. Car 3. Hat 4. Scarf 5. Shoes

Question 6. According to the passage, what needs to be done when painting?

1. Focus 2. Imagine 3. Listen to Music 4. Meditate First 5. Eat

Question 7. According to the passage, the speaker paints in...

1. A Quiet Room 2. A Quiet Library 3. A Loud Playground 4. An Office 5. The Kitchen

Question 8. According to the passage, the quietest time of the day is...

1. Dawn 2. Morning 3. Midnight 4. Afternoon 5. Dinner Time

Question 9. According to the passage, what does the speaker do with his/her paintings?

1. Sell Online 2. Gift To Friends 3. Donate To Charity 4. Keep Them 5. Submit To Art Shows

Question 10. According to the passage, what does the speaker plan on painting?

1. A Cute Rabbit 2. A Scary Monster 3. A Majestic Eagle 4. A Running Cheetah 5. An Adorable Puppy

Question 11. True or False...? Drawing a plant is easier than drawing an animal.

1. True 2. False

Question 12. According to the passage, the reason for the above question is that it...

1. Is Bigger 2. Has More Colors 3. Keeps Moving 4. Is Violent 5. Looks Different

Read the following passage carefully and answer the following questions.

수미가 방에서 울고있습니다.
[su-mi-ga bang-e-seo ul-go-it-seup-ni-da.]

엄마에게 혼났기 때문입니다.
[eom-ma-e-ge hon-nat-gi ttae-mun-ip-ni-da.]

수학 성적이 좋지 않았습니다.
[su-hak seong-jeok-i jot-chi an-at-seup-ni-da.]

수미는 과학을 좋아합니다.
[su-mi-neun gwa-hak-eul jo-a-hap-ni-da.]

그래서 과학 시험은 성적이 좋습니다.
[geu-rae-seo gwa-hak shi-heom-eun seong-jeok-i jot-seup-ni-da.]

수학 공부는 일주일에 세 번 합니다.
[su-hak gong-bu-neun il-ju-il-e se beon hap-ni-da.]

하지만 재미가 없어서 집중하기 어렵습니다.
[ha-ji-man jae-mi-ga eop-seo-seo jip-jung-ha-gi eo-ryeop-seup-ni-da.]

수학 공부를 할 때도, 과학 생각을 합니다.
[su-hak gong-bu-reul hal ttae-do gwa-hak saeng-gak-eul hap-ni-da.]

과학자가 되는 것이 꿈입니다.
[gwa-hak-ja-ga doe-neun geo-shi kkum-ip-ni-da.]

그래서, 미래에 관한 영화를 즐겨 봅니다.
[geu-rae-seo, mi-rae-e gwan-han yeong-hwa-reul jeul-gyeo bop-ni-da.]

미래는 정말 멋질 것 같습니다.
[mi-rae-e-neun jeong-mal meot-jil geot gat-seup-ni-da.]

새로운 직업이 많이 생길 것 같습니다.
[sae-ro-un jik-eop-i man-i saeng-gil geot gat-seup-ni.da.]

Question 1. According to the passage, what is 수미 doing in the room?

1. Singing 2. Laughing 3. Crying 4. Jumping 5. Sleeping

Question 2. According to the passage, why is 수미 doing that?

1. Mom Scolded Her 2. Mom Is Sick 3. Mom Forgot 수미's laundry 4. Mom Is Too Busy

Question 3. According to the passage, why did it happen? Because she (her)...

1. Math Score Wasn't Good 2. Came Home Late 3. Lost Her Wallet 4. Fell Asleep 5. Didn't Study

Question 4. According to the passage, 수미 likes what subject?

1. History 2. Art 3. Math 4. Science 5. P.E.

Question 5. True or False...? 수미's science score wasn't good.

1. True 2. False

Question 6. True or False...? 수미 studies math every day.

1. True 2. False

Question 7. According to the passage, why can't 수미 focus on studying math? Because it's...

1. Not Challenging 2. Not Important 3. Not Easy 4. Not Useful 5. Not Fun

Question 8. According to the passage, what does 수미 do while studying math?

1. Doodle 2. Think About Science 3. Chew Gum 4. Listen To Music 5. Watch TV

Question 9. According to the passage, what does 수미 want to become?

1. A Magician 2. A Science Teacher 3. A Scientist 4. A Dreamer 5. A Drummer

Question 10. According to the passage, what does 수미 do for her dream?

1. Watch Movies About the Future 2. Read Sci-Fi Novel 3. Travel Around 4. Study Hard 5. Learn Skills

Question 11. True or False...? 수미 thinks the future will be gloomy.

1. True 2. False

Question 12. According to the passage, more of THIS will be available in the future?

1. New Jobs 2. New Medicines 3. New Technology 4. New Robots 5. New Clothes

Practice #17 (Difficulty ★ ★ ☆ ☆ ☆)

Read the following passage carefully and answer the following questions.

한국의 역사는 약 사천 오백년 정도입니다.
[han-guk-ui yeok-sa-neun yak sa-cheon o-baek-nyeon jeong-do-ip-ni-da.]

가장 처음 생긴 나라는 고조선입니다.
[ga-jang cheo-eum saeng-gin na-ra-neun go-jo-seon-ip-ni-da.]

고조선을 만든 사람은 단군입니다.
[go-jo-seon-eul man-deun-sa-ram-eun dan-gun-ip-ni-da.]

그때부터, 많은 나라들이 생겼습니다.
[geu-ttae-bu-teo, man-eun na-ra-deul-i saeng-gyeot-seup-ni-da.]

지금은 두 나라로 갈라져있습니다.
[ji-geum-eun du na-ra-ro gal-la-jyeo-it-seup-ni-da.]

전쟁으로 인해 갈라졌습니다.
[jeon-jaeng-eu-ro in-hae gal-la-jyeot-seup-ni-da.]

한국인 모두의 꿈은 통일입니다.
[han-guk-in mo-du-ui kkum-eun tong-il-ip-ni-da.]

그리고, 평화를 원합니다.
[geu-ri-go, pyeong-hwa-reul won-hap-ni-da.]

정치인들이 많은 노력을 해야만 합니다.
[jeong-chi-in-deul-i man-eun no-ryeok-eul hae-ya-man hap-ni-da.]

통일이 되면, 문제보다 기회가 많아질 것 같습니다.
[tong-il-i doe-myeon, mun-je-bo-da gi-hoe-ga man-a-jil geot gat-seup-ni-da.]

그 중에서도, 학교가 많이 필요할 것 같습니다.
[geu jung-e-seo-do, hak-gyo-ga man-i pil-yo-hal geot gat-seup-ni-da.]

새로운 교과서도 만들어야 합니다.
[sae-ro-un gyo-gwa-seo-do man-deul-eo-ya hap-ni-da.]

Question 1. According to the passage, how old is Korean history?

1. About 300 Years 2. About 350 Years 3. About 4,000 Years 4. About 4,500 Years 5. About 5,000 Years

Question 2. According to the passage, what's the name of the first country built?

1. Nara 2. Ga Jang 3. Gojoseon 4. Saeng Gin 5. Cheo Eum

Question 3. According to the passage, who established the country?

1. Sa Ram 2. Man Deun 3. Dan Gun 4. Gojo 5. King Gojoseon

Question 4. True or False...? There have been many countries established since then.

1. True 2. False

Question 5. True or False...? Korea is currently divided into three separate countries.

1. True 2. False

Question 6. True or False...? The reason for the division is differences in the economic system.

1. True 2. False

Question 7. According to the passage, all Koreans dream of...

1. Reunification 2. Eternal Separation 3. Co-operation 4. Democratic Government 5. Immigration

Question 8. According to the passage, what else do Koreans want?

1. Peace 2. Harmony 3. Joy 4. Co-operation 5. Mutual Understanding

Question 9. According to the passage, who needs to try harder for it to happen?

1. Politicians 2. Students 3. Corporations 4. Military Officers 5. United Nations

Question 10. True or False...? The speaker thinks there will be more troubles than opportunities once reunified.

1. True 2. False

Question 11. According to the speaker, THIS will be needed more than anything else.

1. Hospitals 2. Police Stations 3. Military Bases 4. Restaurants 5. Schools

Question 12. According to the speaker, what else is needed to be made?

1. New Textbooks 2. New Schools 3. New Language 4. New TV Stations 5. New National Anthem

Practice #18 (Difficulty ★ ★ ☆ ☆ ☆)

Read the following passage carefully and answer the following questions.

저는 일년에 두 번씩 여행을 갑니다.
[jeo-neun il-nyeon-e du beon-ssik yeo-haeng-eul gap-ni-da.]

여름과 겨울에 갑니다.
[yeo-reum-gwa gyeo-ul-e gap-ni-da.]

그때는 방학이기 때문입니다.
[geu-ttae-neun bang-hak-i-gi ttae-mun-ip-ni-da.]

아직 많은 나라를 가보지는 못했습니다.
[a-jik man-eun na-ra-reul ga-bo-ji-neun mot-haet-seup-ni-da.]

여행을 갈 때는 혼자 가는 것을 좋아합니다.
[yeo-haeng-eul gal ttae-neun hon-jsa ga-neun geo-seul jo-a-hap-ni-da.]

천천히 구경하는 것이 편하기 때문입니다.
[cheon-cheon-hi gu-gyeong-ha-neun geo-shi pyeon-ha-gi ttae-mun-ip-ni-da.]

풍경 사진을 찍는 것을 좋아합니다.
[pung-gyeong sa-jin-eul jjik-neun geo-seul jo-a-hap-ni-da.]

아름다운 자연을 보면, 마음이 편해집니다.
[a-reum-da-un ja-yeon-eul bo-myeon, ma-eum-i pyeon-hae-jip-ni-da.]

비행기를 타는 것은 무섭지만, 잠을 자면서 가면 괜찮습니다.
[bi-haeng-gi-reul ta-neun geo-seun mu-seop-ji-man, jam-eul ja-myeon-seo ga-myeon goen-chan-seup-ni-da.]

더 많은 나라를 여행하기 위해서, 영어를 공부 할 것입니다.
[deo man-eun na-ra-reul yeo-haeng-ha-gi wi-hae-seo, yeong-eo-reul gong-bu hal geo-ship-ni-da.]

다양한 나라의 친구들을 만나고 싶습니다.
[da-yang-han na-ra-ui chin-gu-deul-eul man-na-go ship-seup-ni-da.]

오늘부터 열심히 돈을 모을 것입니다.
[o-neul-bu-teo yeol-shim-bi don-eul mo-eul geo-ship-ni-da.]

Question 1. According to the passage, how often does the speaker travel?

1. Once Every Year 2. Twice Every Year 3. Three Times Every Year 4. Once Every Two Years

Question 2. According to the passage, when does the speaker travel?

1. Spring and Summer 2. Spring and Autumn 3. Summer and Autumn 4. Summer and Winter

Question 3. According to the passage, the speaker travels during that time because it's/of...

1. School Break 2. Holiday Season 3. Cheap To Travel 4. Less Crowded 5. Safer To Travel

Question 4. True or False...? The speaker has been to many different countries.

1. True 2. False

Question 5. True or False...? The speaker prefers to travel alone

1. True 2. False

Question 6. True or False...? The reason for the above is that the speaker wants a quick tour.

1. True 2. False

Question 7. According to the passage, the speaker likes to take photos of...

1. Landscape 2. People 3. Animals 4. Buildings 5. Markets

Question 8. According to the passage, seeing beautiful nature makes the speaker feel...

1. Excited 2. Calm 3. Comfortable 4. Generous 5. Grateful

Question 9. According to the passage, what does the speaker do during a flight?

1. Sleep 2. Watch Movie 3. Drink Wine 4. Study 5. Listen To Music

Question 10. According to the passage, the speaker plans to study THIS to travel to more countries.

1. Geography 2. World History 3. English 4. Art 5. Korean

Question 11. According to the passage, the speaker wants to do THIS.

1. Meet Friends From Various Countries 2. Make a Photo Album 3. Write a Novel 4. Start a Tour Company

Question 12. According to the passage, the speaker will do THIS starting today.

1. Save Money 2. Study Hard 3. Learn To Cook 4. Exercise 5. Read More Novels

Practice #19 (Difficulty ★ ★ ☆ ☆ ☆)

Read the following passage carefully and answer the following questions.

일년 중 가장 추운 때는 십이월입니다.
[il nyeon jung ga-jang chu-un ttae-neun shib-i-wol-ip-ni-da.]

온도가 영하 십오도 까지 내려갑니다.
[on-do-ga yeong-ha ship-o-do kka-ji nae-ryeo-gap-ni-da.]

눈은 자주 오지 않지만, 올 경우에는 많이 옵니다.
[nun-eun ja-ju o-ji an-chi-man, ol gyeong-u-e-neun man-i-op-ni-da.]

반대로, 가장 더운 때는 팔월입니다.
[ban-dae-ro, ga-jang deo-un ttae-neun pal-wol-ip-ni-da.]

온도가 삼십 팔도까지 올라갑니다.
[on-do-ga sam-ship pal-do-kka-ji ol-la-gap-ni-da.]

가장 추운 곳은 강원도입니다.
[ga-jang chu-un-go-seun gang-won-do-ip-ni-da.]

산이 많아 더욱 춥습니다.
[san-i man-a deo-uk chup-seup-ni-da.]

여름에 인기 있는 관광지는 제주도입니다.
[yeo-reum-e in-gi it-neun gwan-gwang-ji-neun je-ju-do-ip-ni-da.]

춥지도 않고, 덥지도 않아서입니다.
[chup-ji-do an-go, deop-ji-do an-a-seo-ip-ni-da.]

다양한 해산물도 먹을 수 있습니다.
[da-yang-han hae-san-mul-do meok-eul su it-seup-ni-da.]

그리고, 아름다운 바다를 구경할 수 있습니다.
[geu-ri-go, a-reum-da-un ba-da-reul gu-gyeong-hal-su it-seup-ni-da.]

제주도는 굉장히 이국적인 곳입니다.
[je-ju-do-neun goeng-jang-hi i-guk-jeok-in got-ip-ni-da.]

Question 1. According to the passage, when is the coldest time of the year?

1. January 2. April 3. June 4. October 5. December

Question 2. According to the passage, how low can the temperature go?

1. -10 2. -13 3. -15 4. -18 5. -20

Question 3. True or False...? It doesn't snow often during the time.

1. True 2. False

Question 4. True or False...? When is the hottest time of the year?

1. March 2. May 3. June 4. July 5. August

Question 5. According to the passage, how high can the temperature go?

1. 25 2. 32 3. 35 4. 38 5. 42

Question 6. According to the passage, where is the coldest place?

1. Ganghwado 2. Gangwondo 3. Gyeonggido 4. Gangdo 5. Gangseogu

Question 7. According to the passage, the reason it's so cold there is that there are many...

1. Mountains 2. Beaches 3. Open Spaces 4. Ice Bergs 5. Trees

Question 8. True or False...? Jejudo is the most popular place during the summer.

1. True 2. False

Question 9. According to the passage, it is because the weather is...

1. Humid 2. Dry 3. Neither Not Cold nor Hot 4. Both Cold and Hot 5. Unpredictable

Question 10. According to the passage, what can you eat in Jejudo?

1. Various Seafood 2. Various Sushi 3. Various Steaks 4. Traditional Dishes 5. Fresh Dairy

Question 11. According to the passage, you can also see THIS in Jejudo.

1. Beautiful Sea 2. Amazing Sunset 3. Splendid Mountains 4. Unique Stones 5. Traditional Houses

Question 12. According to the passage, what kind of place is Jejudo?

1. Excellent 2. Exotic 3. Romantic 4. Lovely 5. Close

Read the following passage carefully and answer the following questions.

서울에서 부산까지 갈 수 있는 방법은 여러가지입니다.
[seo-ul-e-seo bu-san-kka-ji gal su it-neun bang-beop-eun yeo-reo-ga-ji-ip-ni-da.]

자동차, 기차, 비행기로 가능합니다.
[ja-dong-cha, gi-cha, bi-haeng-gi-ro ga-neung-hap-ni-da.]

자동차는 다섯 시간, 기차는 세 시간, 비행기는 한 시간 걸립니다.
[ja-dong-cha-neun da-seot shi-gan, gi-cha-neun se shi-gan, bi-haeng-gi-neun han shi-gan geol-lip-ni-da.]

저는 비행기로 가는 것을 가장 선호합니다.
[jeo-neun bi-haeng-gi-ro ga-neun geo-seul ga-jang seon-ho-hap-ni-da.]

빨리 도착해서 친구들을 만날 수 있으니까요.
[bbal-li do-chak-hae-seo chin-gu-deul-eul man-nal su i-seu-ni-kka-yo.]

하지만 비행기는 가장 비쌉니다.
[ha-ji-man bi-haeng-gi-neun ga-jang bi-ssap-ni-da.]

자동차는 가장 저렴합니다.
[ja-dong-cha-neun ga-jang jeo-ryeom-hap-ni-da.]

운전을 오래 하면, 정말 피곤합니다.
[un-jeon-eul o-rae ha-myeon, jeong-mal pi-gon-hap-ni-da.]

가끔씩 멈춰서, 휴식을 해야 합니다.
[ga-kkeum-ssik meom-chwo-seo, hyu-sik-eul hae-ya hap-ni-da.]

휴게소에는 다양한 음식이 있습니다.
[hyu-ge-so-e-neun da-yang-han eum-sik-i it-seup-ni-da.]

그 중에서도, 김밥이 가장 인기가 있습니다.
[geu jung-e-seo-do, gim-bap-i ga-jang in-gi-ga it-seup-ni-da.]

먹기 편하기 때문입니다.
[meok-gi pyeon-ha-gi ttae-mun-ip-ni-da.]

Question 1. True or False...? There is only one transportation method available between Seoul and Busan.

1. True 2. False

Question 2. According to the passage, which of the following is NOT a transportation method available between Seoul and Busan?

1. Car 2. Train 3. Airplane 4. Subway

Question 3. True or False...? Train takes the most amount of time.

1. True 2. False

Question 4. According to the passage, the speaker prefers WHICH transportation method?

1. Car 2. Bus 3. Train 4. Airplane 5. Ship

Question 5. According to the passage, the benefit of doing the above is...?

1. Safety 2. Can Arrive Early and Meet Friends 3. Can Arrive Anytime You Want 4. Can Sleep Well

Question 6. True or False...? Airplane is the most expensive transportation option.

1. True 2. False

Question 7. True or False...? Car is the most expensive transportation option.

1. True 2. False

Question 8. According to the passage, THIS for a long time is really tiring.

1. Driving 2. Singing 3. Riding on a Bus 4. Flying on an Airplane 5. Walking

Question 9. According to the passage, you need to do THIS while driving.

1. Stop and Rest 2. Study The Road 3. Listen To News Channel 4. Check Location 5. Focus

Question 10. According to the passage, service stations offer various kinds of THIS...

1. Food 2. Souvenir 3. Drink 4. Book 5. T-Shirt

Question 11. According to the passage, what food is most popular?

1. Kimbap 2. Kimchi 3. Fried Rice 4. Ramyeon Noodles 5. Rice Bowl

Question 12. According to the passage, it is popular because it is...

1. Easy to Eat 2. Inexpensive 3. Safe For Babies 4. Made with Natural Ingredients 5. Portable

Practice #11

저는 다음 달에 한국에 갑니다.
I'm going to Korea next month.
[jeo-neun da-eum dal-e han-guk-e gap-ni-da.]
한국에는 세 번 가 본 적이 있습니다.
I've been to Korea three times.
[han-guk-e-neun se beon ga bon jeok-i it-seup-ni-da.]
여름에 두 번, 겨울에 한 번 가봤습니다.
Twice in the Summer, and three times in the Winter.
[yeo-reum-e du-beon, gyeo-ul-e han beon ga-bwat-seup-ni-da.]
저는 겨울보다는 여름에 가는 것이 좋았습니다.
I liked going there in the Summer more than in the Winter.
[jeo-neun gyeo-ul-bo-da-neun yeo-reum-e ga-neun geo-shi so-at-seup-ni-da.]
겨울에는 날씨가 추워서 밖에 나가기가 힘들었습니다.
In the Winter, it was difficult to go out because it was too cold.
[gyeo-ul-e-neun nal-ssi-ga chu-wo-seo bak-e na-ga-gi-ga him-deul-eot-seup-ni-da.]
제가 살고 있는 곳 보다 많이 춥습니다.
It's a lot colder than where I live.
[je-ga sal-go it-neun dok-il-bo-da man-i chup-seup-ni-da.]
제가 가장 좋아한 곳은 박물관 입니다.
The place I liked the most is the museum.
[je-ga ga-jang jo-a-han go-seun bak-mul-gwan ip-ni-da.]
한국의 미술에 관심이 많기 때문입니다.
It's because I'm very interested in Korean art.
[han-guk-eui mi-sul-e gwan-shim-i man-ki ttae-mun-ip-ni-da.]
한국의 불교 미술은 정말 아름답습니다.
 Korean Buddhism art is really beautiful.
[han-guk-eui bul-gyo mi-sul-eun jeong-mal a-reum-dap-seup-ni-da.]
그래서, 한국 미술을 공부할 계획입니다.
So I plan to study Korean art.
[geu-rae-seo, han-guk mi-sul-eul gong-bu-hal gye-hoek-ip-ni-da.]
한국의 미술을 독일 친구들에게 알리고 싶습니다.
I'd like to promote Korean art to my German friends.
[han-guk-eui mi-sul-eul dok-il chin-gu-deul-e-ge al-li-go ship-seup-ni-da.]
공부를 많이 해서, 한국 미술 전문가가 되고 싶습니다. I'd like to study a lot and become a Korean art expert.
[gong-bu-reul man-i hae-seo, han-guk mi-sul jeon-mun-ga-ga doe-go ship-seup-ni-da.]

Answer Keys : (1) 3 (2) 3 (3) 2 (4) 1 (5) 2 (6) 2 (7) 1 (8) 2
(9) 4 (10) 1 (11) 1 (12) 4

Practice #12

한국에는 맛있는 음식이 많습니다.
There are lots of tasty foods in Korea.
[han-guk-e-neun ma-shit-neun eum-shik-i man-seup-ni-da.]
저는 아직 많은 한국 음식을 먹어보지 못했습니다.
I haven't tried a lot of Korean foods yet.
[jeo-neun a-jik man-eun han-guk eum-shik-eul.meok-eo-bo-ji mot-haet-seup-ni-da.]
하지만 먹어본 것 중에서는 비빔밥을 좋아합니다.
But of the ones I tried, I like bibimbap.

[ha-ji-man meok-eo-bon geot jung-e-seo-neun bi-bim-bap-eul jo-a-hap-ni-da.]
다양한 재료가 들어있어, 영양소가 많습니다.
There are a variety of ingredients, so it has a lot of nutrition.
[da-yang-han jae-ryo-ga deul-eo-it-sseo, yeong-yang-so-ga man-seup-ni-da.]
비빔밥은 한국의 전통 음식입니다.
Bibimbap is a traditional food in Korea.
[bi-bim-bap-eun han-guk-eui jeon-tong eum-shik-ip-ni-da.]
왕과 일반인 모두 먹을 수 있었습니다.
 King and the common people could all eat it.
[wang-gwa il-ban-in mo-du meok-eul su it-sseot-seup-ni-da.]
이제 비빔밥은 세계적인 음식이 되었습니다.
 Now bibimbap has become an international food.
[i-je bi-bim-bap-eum se-gye-jeok-in eum-shik-i doe-eot-sseup-ni-da.]
외국인들도 비빔밥을 즐깁니다.
 Foreigners enjoy Bimbimbap too.
[oe-guk-in-deul-do bi-bim-bap-eul jeul-gip-ni-da.]
외국인들은 고추장을 넣지 않고 먹기도 합니다.
Foreigners also eat it without putting gochujang.
[oe-guk-in-deul-eun go-chu-jang-eul neot-ji an-go meok-gi-do hap-ni-da.]
외국인들에게는 너무 맵기 때문입니다.
 It's because it's too spicy for foreigners.
[oe-guk-in-deul-e-ge-neun neo-mu maep-gi ttae-mun-ip-ni-da.]
하지만 저는 고추장을 많이 넣어 먹습니다.
But I eat it with lots of gochujang put in.
[ha-ji-man jeo-neun go-chu-jang-eul man-i neo-eo meok-seup-ni-da.]
저는 매운 한국 음식을 좋아하기 때문입니다.
It's because I like spicy Korean food.
[jeo-neun mae-un han-guk eum-shik-eul jo-a-ha-gi ttae-mun-ip-ni-da.]

Answer Keys : (1) 1 (2) 2 (3) 1 (4) 1 (5) 2 (6) 2 (7) 1 (8) 1
(9) 4 (10) 2 (11) 1 (12) 1

Practice #13

수요일과 금요일은 한국어 공부를 하는 날 입니다.
Wednesdays and Fridays are Korean study days.
[su-yo-il-gwa geum-yo-il-eun han-guk-eo gong-bu-reul ha-neun nal ip-ni-da]
저희 한국어 선생님은 나이가 많으십니다.
Our Korean teacher is quite old.
[jeo-hui han-guk-eo seon-saeng-nim-eun na-i-ga man-eu-ship-ni-da.]
따라서, 경험이 많으십니다.
Therefore, he/she has lots of experience.
[tta-ra-seo, gyeong-heom-i man-eu-ship-ni-da.]
수업시간에는 매일 한국어 속담을 가르쳐 주십니다.
During the class, he/she teaches us a Korean saying every day.
[su-eop-shi-gan-e-neun mae-il han-guk-eo sok-dam-eul ga-reu-chyeo ju-ship-ni-da.]
한국의 역사와 문화에 대해 많이 아십니다.
He/she knows a lot about Korean history and culture.
[han-guk-ui yeok-sa-wa mun-hwa-e dae-hae man-i a-ship-ni-da.]

수업시간은 다양한 국적의 학생들이 있습니다.
Class time has students from a variety of nationalities.
[su-eop-shi-gan-eun da-yang-han guk-jeok-ui hak-saeng-deul-i it-seup-ni-da.]
미국 학생이 가장 많고, 독일 학생은 한 명입니다.
We have American students the most, and there is only one German student.
[mi-guk hak-saeng-i ga-jang man-ko, dok-il hak-saeng-eun han myeong-ip-ni-da.]
아침 열 시 부터 오후 두 시 까지 수업입니다.
From ten in the morning to two in the afternoon is the class.
[a-chim yeol shi bu-teo o-hu du shi kka-ji su-eop-ip-ni-da.]
점심에는 모두 같이 모여서 식사를 합니다.
During lunch time, we all get together and have a meal.
[jeom-shim-e-neun mo-du ga-chi mo-yeo-seo shik-sa-reul hap-ni-da.]
주로 한국 연예인 이야기를 많이 합니다.
We mostly talk about Korean entertainers.
[ju-ro han-guk yeon-ye-in i-ya-gi-reul man-i hap-ni-da.]
앞으로 약 육개월 정도 수업을 더 들어야 합니다.
We need to take the class for about six more months.
[ap-eu-ro yak yuk-gae-wol jeong-do su-eop-eul deo deul-eo-ya hap-ni-da.]
수업을 다 듣고, 친구들과 함께 제주도로 여행을 갈 예정입니다. After taking all the classes, I plan to take a trip to Jejudo with my friends.
[su-eop-eul da deut-go, chin-gu-deul-gwa ham-kke je-ju-do-ro yeo-haeng-eul gal ye-jeong-ip-ni-da.]

Answer Keys : (1) 5 (2) 2 (3) 5 (4) 2 (5) 3 (6) 2 (7) 1 (8) 3
(9) 2 (10) 1 (11) 4 (12) 1

Practice #14

오늘은 눈이 많이 내린 하루였습니다.
Today was a day with a lot of snow falling.
[o-neul-eun nun-i man-i nae-rin ha-ru-yeot-seup-ni-da.]
오전부터 계속해서 내렸습니다.
It has continued to snow since the morning.
[o-jeon-bu-teo gye-sok-hae-seo nae-ryeot-seup-ni-da.]
저녁이 되어서야 멈췄습니다.
It stopped only when it became night.
[jeo-nyeok-i doe-eo-seo-ya meom-chwot-seup-ni-da.]
오전보다 오후에 눈이 더 많이 내렸습니다.
It snowed more in the afternoon than in the morning.
[o-jeon-bo-da o-hu-e nun-i deo-man-i nae-ryeot-seup-ni-da.]
많은 사람들이 길에서 넘어졌습니다.
A lot of people fell on the street.
[man-eun sa-ram-deul-i gil-e-seo neom-eo-jyeot-seup-ni-da.]
평소보다 지하철을 이용하는 사람들이 많았습니다.
There were more people using the subway than usual.
[pyeong-so-bo-da ji-ha-cheol-eul i-yong-ha-neun sa-ram-deul-i man-at-seup-ni-da.]
다행히도, 눈이 쌓이지는 않았습니다.
Luckily, the snow didn't accumulate.
[da-haeng-hi-do, nun-i ssa-i-ji-neun an-at-seup-ni-da.]
내일은 날씨가 따뜻할 것이라고 합니다.
It's been told that it will be warm tomorrow.
[nae-il-eun nal-ssi-ga tta-tteut-hal geo-shi-ra-go hap-ni-da.]

집에서 나오기 전에, 항상 날씨를 확인해야합니다.
Before getting out of home, you must always check the weather.
[jib-e-seo na-o-gi jeon-e, hang-sang nal-ssi-reul hwak-in-hae-ya-hap-ni-da.]
그리고, 작은 우산을 들고 다녀야합니다.
And, you should carry a small umbrella.
[geu-ri-go, jak-eun u-san-eul deul-go da-nyeo-ya-hap-ni-da.]
온도의 차이가 심해서, 감기에 걸리기 쉽습니다.
Because the temperature difference is huge, it's easy to catch a cold.
[on-do-eui cha-i-ga shim-hae-seo, gam-gi-e geol-li-gi ship-seup-ni-da.]
감기에 걸리면, 곧바로 병원에 가야합니다.
If you catch a cold, you have to go to the hospital immediately.
[gam-gi-e geol-li-myeon, got-ba-ro byeong-won-e ga-ya-hap-ni-da.]

Answer Keys : (1) 4 (2) 1 (3) 2 (4) 2 (5) 1 (6) 1 (7) 5 (8) 1
(9) 2 (10) 2 (11) 2 (12) 4

Practice #15

저의 꿈은 화가가 되는 것입니다.
My dream is to become a painter.
[jeo-eui kkum-eun hwa-ga-ga doe-neun geo-ship-ni-da.]
어려서부터 그림을 그리는 것을 좋아했습니다. I liked drawing/painting since I was little.
[eo-ryeo-seo-bu-teo geu-ri-neun geo-seul jo-a-haet-seup-ni-da.]
많은 색 중에서 저는 분홍색을 가장 좋아합니다.
Among many colors, I like pink the most.
[man-eun saek jung-e-seo jeo-neun bun-hong-saek-eul ga-jang jo-a-hap-ni-da.]
분홍색을 보면 기분이 좋아집니다.
Looking at pink color makes me feel good.
[bun-hong-saek-eul bo-myeon gi-bun-i jo-a-jip-ni-da.]
그래서 분홍색의 옷을 좋아합니다.
So I like pink clothes.
[geu-rae-seo bun-hong-saek-eui o-seul jo-a-hap-ni-da.]
그림을 그릴때에는 집중을 해야합니다.
When drawing/painting, I need to focus.
[geu-rim-eul geu-ril-ttae-e-neun jip-jung-eul hae-ya-hap-ni-da.]
그래서 조용한 방에서 그림을 그립니다.
So I draw/paint in a quiet room.
[geu-rae-seo jo-yong-han bang-e-seo geu-rim-eul geu-rip-ni-da.]
모두 잠이 든 새벽이 가장 조용합니다.
Dawn when everyone has fallen asleep is the quietest.
[mo-du jam-i deun sae-byeok-i ga-jang jo-yong-hap-ni-da.]
아름다운 그림을 그려서, 친구들에게 선물합니다.
I draw/paint beautiful paintings and gift them to friends.
[a-reum-da-un geu-rim-eul geu-ryeo-seo, chin-gu-deul-e-ge seon-mul-hap-ni-da.]
이번에는 귀여운 토끼를 그릴 계획입니다.
This time, I plan to draw/paint a cute bunny.
[i-beon-e-neun gwi-yeo-un to-kki-reul geu-ril-gye-hoek-ip-ni-da.]
동물을 그리는 것은 식물을 그리는 것 보다 어렵습니다.
Drawing/painting an animal is more difficult than drawing/painting a plant.

[dong-mul-eul geu-ri-neun geo-seun shik-mul-eul geu-ri-neun geot bo-da eo-ryeop-seup-ni-da.]
계속해서 움직이기 때문입니다.
It's because they keep moving.
[gye-sok-hae-seo um-jik-i-gi tae-mun-ip-ni-da.]

Answer Keys : (1) 1 (2) 1 (3) 5 (4) 1 (5) 1 (6) 1 (7) 1 (8) 1
(9) 2 (10) 1 (11) 1 (12) 3

Practuce #16

수미가 방에서 울고있습니다.
Sumi is crying alone in the room.
[su-mi-ga bang-e-seo ul-go-it-seup-ni-da.]
엄마에게 혼났기 때문입니다.
It's because her mom told her off.
[eom-ma-e-ge hon-nat-gi tae-mun-ip-ni-da.]
수학 성적이 좋지 않았습니다.
Math grade was not good.
[su-hak seong-jeok-i jot-chi an-at-seup-ni-da.]
수미는 과학을 좋아합니다.
Sumi likes science.
[su-mi-neun gwa-hak-eul jo-a-hap-ni-da.]
그래서 과학 시험은 성적이 좋습니다.
So science grade is good.
[geu-rae-seo gwa-hak shi-heom-eun seong-jeok-i jot-seup-ni-da.]
수학 공부는 일주일에 세 번 합니다.
 (Sumi) studies math three times a week.
[su-hak gong-bu-neun il-ju-il-e se beon hap-ni-da.]
하지만 재미가 없어서 집중하기 어렵습니다.
But it's difficult to focus because it's not fun.
[ha-ji-man jae-mi-ga eop-seo-seo jip-jung-ha-gi eo-ryeop-seup-ni-da.]
수학 공부를 할 때도, 과학 생각을 합니다.
Even while studying math, (she) thinks about science.
[su-hak gong-bu-reul hal ttae-do gwa-hak saeng-gak-eul hap-ni-da.]
과학자가 되는 것이 꿈입니다.
Being a scientist is (her) dream.
[gwa-hak-ja-ga doe-neun geo-shi kkum-ip-ni-da.]
그래서, 미래에 관한 영화를 즐겨 봅니다.
So she enjoys watching movies about the future.
[geu-rae-seo, mi-rae-e gwan-han yeong-hwa-reul jeul-gyeo bop-ni-da.]
미래는 정말 멋질 것 같습니다.
I think the future will be really cool.
[mi-rae-e-neun jeong-mal meot-jil geot gat-seup-ni-da.]
새로운 직업이 많이 생길 것 같습니다.
I think there will be lots of new jobs.
[sae-ro-un jik-eop-i man-i saeng-gil geot gat-seup-ni-da.]

Answer Keys : (1) 3 (2) 1 (3) 1 (4) 4 (5) 2 (6) 2 (7) 5 (8) 2
(9) 3 (10) 1 (11) 2 (12) 1

Practice #17

한국의 역사는 약 사천 오백년 정도입니다.
Korean history is about four thousand and five hundred years.
 [han-guk-ui yeok-sa-neun yak sa-cheon o-baek-nyeon jeong-do-ip-ni-da.]
가장 처음 생긴 나라는 고조선입니다.
The very first country ever appeared was Gojoseon.
 [ga-jang cheo-eum saeng-gin na-ra-neun go-jo-seon-ip-ni-da.]
고조선을 만든 사람은 단군입니다.
The person who created (founded) Gojoseon is Dangun.
 [go-jo-seon-eul man-deun-sa-ram-eun dan-gun-ip-ni-da.]
그때부터, 많은 나라들이 생겼습니다.
Since then, lots of countries have come into existence.
 [geu-ttae-bu-teo, man-eun na-ra-deul-i saeng-gyeot-seup-ni-da.]
지금은 두 나라로 갈라져있습니다.
Now it's been divided into two countries.
 [ji-geum-eun du na-ra-ro gal-la-jyeo-it-seup-ni-da.]
전쟁으로 인해 갈라졌습니다.
It's been divided due to war.
 [jeon-jaeng-eu-ro in-hae gal-la-jyeot-seup-ni-da.]
한국인 모두의 꿈은 통일입니다.
 Every Korean's dream is unification.
 [han-guk-in mo-du-ui kkum-eun tong-il-ip-ni-da.]
그리고, 평화를 원합니다.
And they want peace.
 [geu-ri-go, pyeong-hwa-reul won-hap-ni-da.]
정치인들이 많은 노력을 해야만 합니다.
Politicians need to put a lot of effort.
 [jeong-chi-in-deul-i man-eun no-ryeok-eul hae-ya-man hap-ni-da.]
통일이 되면, 문제보다 기회가 많아질 것 같습니다.
If unified, it seems like there will be more opportunities than problems.
 [tong-il-i doe-myeon, mun-je-bo-da gi-hoe-ga man-a-jil geot gat-seup-ni-da.]
그 중에서도, 학교가 많이 필요할 것 같습니다.
Among those, it seems like lots of schools will be needed.
 [geu jung-e-seo-do, hak-gyo-ga man-i pil-yo-hal geot gat-seup-ni-da.]
새로운 교과서도 만들어야 합니다.
New textbooks must be made too.
 [sae-ro-un gyo-gwa-seo-do man-deul-eo-ya hap-ni-da.]

Answer Keys : (1) 4 (2) 3 (3) 3 (4) 1 (5) 2 (6) 2 (7) 1 (8) 1
(9) 1 (10) 2 (11) 5 (12) 1

Practice #18

저는 일년에 두 번씩 여행을 갑니다.
I go on a trip twice a year.
[jeo-neun il-nyeon-e du beon-ssik yeo-haeng-eul gap-ni-da.]
여름과 겨울에 갑니다.
I go in the Summer and in the Winter.
[yeo-reum-gwa gyeo-ul-e gap-ni-da.]
그때는 방학이기 때문입니다.
It's because it's break time then.
[geu-ttae-neun bang-hak-i-gi ttae-mun-ip-ni-da.]
아직 많은 나라를 가보지는 못했습니다.
I haven't been to many countries yet.
[a-jik man-eun na-ra-reul ga-bo-ji-neun mot-haet-seup-ni-da.]
여행을 갈 때는 혼자 가는 것을 좋아합니다.
I prefer going alone when I travel.
[yeo-haeng-eul gal ttae-neun hon-jsa ga-neun geo-seul jo-a-hap-ni-da.]
천천히 구경하는 것이 편하기 때문입니다.

It's because it's more comfortable looking at things slowly.
[cheon-cheon-hi gu-gyeong-ha-neun geo-shi pyeon-ha-gi ttae-mun-ip-ni-da.]
풍경 사진을 찍는 것을 좋아합니다.
I enjoy taking photos of the scenery.
[pung-gyeong sa-jin-eul jjik-neun geo-seul jo-a-hap-ni-da.]
아름다운 자연을 보면, 마음이 편해집니다.
If I look at beautiful nature, my mind becomes relaxed.
[a-reum-da-un ja-yeon-eul bo-myeon, ma-eum-i pyeon-hae-jip-ni-da.]
비행기를 타는 것은 무섭지만, 잠을 자면서 가면 괜찮습니다.
Taking a plane is scary, but it's okay if you sleep while going.
[bi-haeng-gi-reul ta-neun geo-seun mu-seop-ji-man, jam-eul ja-myeon-seo ga-myeon goen-chan-seup-ni-da.]
더 많은 나라를 여행하기 위해서, 영어를 공부 할 것입니다.
In order to travel to more countries, I am going to study English.
[deo man-eun na-ra-reul yeo-haeng-ha-gi wi-hae-seo, yeong-eo-reul gong-bu hal geo-ship-ni-da.]
다양한 나라의 친구들을 만나고 싶습니다.
I want to meet friends from various countries.
[da-yang-han na-ra-ui chin-gu-deul-eul man-na-go ship-seup-ni-da.]
오늘부터 열심히 돈을 모을 것입니다.
I will save up money zealously starting today.
[o-neul-bu-teo yeol-shim-bi don-eul mo-eul geo-ship-ni-da.]

Answer Keys : (1) 2 (2) 4 (3) 1 (4) 2 (5) 1 (6) 2 (7) 1 (8) 2
(9) 1 (10) 3 (11) 1 (12) 1

Practice #19

일년 중 가장 추운 때는 십이월입니다.
The coldest time of the year is December.
[il nyeon jung ga-jang chu-un ttae-neun shib-i-wol-ip-ni-da.]
온도가 영하 십오도 까지 내려갑니다.
The temperature goes down to minus fifteen degrees.
[on-do-ga yeong-ha ship-o-do kka-ji nae-ryeo-gap-ni-da.]
눈은 자주 오지 않지만, 올 경우에는 많이 옵니다.
 It doesn't snow often, but when it does, it snows a lot.
[nun-eun ja-ju o-ji an-chi-man, ol gyeong-u-e-neun man-i-op-ni-da.]
반대로, 가장 더운 때는 팔월입니다.
 Conversely, the hottest time of the year is August.
[ban-dae-ro, ga-jang deo-un ttae-neun pal-wol-ip-ni-da.]
온도가 삼십 팔도까지 올라갑니다.
The temperature goes up to thirty-eight degrees.
[on-do-ga sam-ship pal-do-kka-ji ol-la-gap-ni-da.]
가장 추운 곳은 강원도입니다.
The coldest place is Gangwondo.
[ga-jang chu-un-go-seun gang-won-do-ip-ni-da.]
산이 많아 더욱 춥습니다.
 It's colder because there are many mountains.
[san-i man-a deo-uk chup-seup-ni-da.]
여름에 인기 있는 관광지는 제주도입니다.
The most popular tourist spot is Jejudo.
[yeo-reum-e in-gi it-neun gwan-gwang-ji-neun je-ju-do-ip-ni-da.]

춥지도 않고, 덥지도 않아서입니다.
It's because it's not cold or hot.
[chup-ji-do an-go, deop-ji-do an-a-seo-ip-ni-da.]
다양한 해산물도 먹을 수 있습니다.
You can also eat various seafoods.
[da-yang-han hae-san-mul-do meok-eul su it-seup-ni-da.]
그리고, 아름다운 바다를 구경할 수 있습니다.
And, you can see a beautiful sea.
[geu-ri-go, a-reum-da-un ba-da-reul gu-gyeong-hal-su it-seup-ni-da.]
제주도는 굉장히 이국적인 곳입니다.
Jejudo is a very exotic place.
[je-ju-do-neun goeng-jang-hi i-guk-jeok-in got-ip-ni-da.]

Answer Keys : (1) 5 (2) 3 (3) 1 (4) 5 (5) 4 (6) 2 (7) 1 (8) 2
(9) 3 (10) 1 (11) 1 (12) 2

Practice #20

서울에서 부산까지 갈 수 있는 방법은 여러가지입니다.
There are many ways to get to Busan from Seoul.
[seo-ul-e-seo bu-san-kka-ji gal su it-neun bang-beop-eun yeo-reo-ga-ji-ip-ni-da.]
자동차, 기차, 비행기로 가능합니다.
It's possible by car, train, and airplane.
[ja-dong-cha, gi-cha, bi-haeng-gi-ro ga-neung-hap-ni-da.]
자동차는 다섯 시간, 기차는 세 시간, 비행기는 한 시간 걸립니다. It takes five hours by car, three hours by train, and one hour by plane.
[ja-dong-cha-neun da-seot shi-gan, gi-cha-neun se shi-gan, bi-haeng-gi-neun han shi-gan geol-lip-ni-da.]
저는 비행기로 가는 것을 가장 선호합니다.
I prefer going by airplane the most.
[jeo-neun bi-haeng-gi-ro ga-neun geo-seul ga-jang seon-ho-hap-ni-da.]
빨리 도착해서 친구들을 만날 수 있으니까요.
Because I can get there fast and meet friends.
[bbal-li do-chak-hae-seo chin-gu-deul-eul man-nal su i-seu-ni-kka-yo.]
하지만 비행기는 가장 비쌉니다.
But airplanes are the most expensive.
[ha-ji-man bi-haeng-gi-neun ga-jang bi-ssap-ni-da.]
자동차는 가장 저렴합니다. Cars are the cheapest.
[ja-dong-cha-neun ga-jang jeo-ryeom-hap-ni-da.]
운전을 오래 하면, 정말 피곤합니다.
If I drive for too long, it's really tiring.
[un-jeon-eul o-rae ha-myeon, jeong-mal pi-gon-hap-ni-da.]
가끔씩 멈춰서, 휴식을 해야 합니다.
Sometimes you need to stop and take a break.
[ga-kkeum-ssik meom-chwo-seo, hyu-sik-eul hae-ya hap-ni-da.]
휴게소에는 다양한 음식이 있습니다.
Service stations have various foods.
[hyu-ge-so-e-neun da-yang-han eum-sik-i it-seup-ni-da.]
그 중에서도, 김밥이 가장 인기가 있습니다.
Among all, Kimbap is the most popular.
[geu jung-e-seo-do, gim-bap-i ga-jang in-gi-ga it-seup-ni-da.]
먹기 편하기 때문입니다.
It's because it's convenient to eat.
[meok-gi pyeon-ha-gi ttae-mun-ip-ni-da.]

Answer Keys : (1) 2 (2) 4 (3) 2 (4) 4 (5) 2 (6) 1 (7) 2 (8) 1
(9) 1 (10) 1 (11) 1 (12) 1

Read the following passage carefully and answer the following questions.

올 해 부터는 많은 것들이 달라집니다.
[ol hae bu-teo-neun man-eun geot-deul-i dal-la-jip-ni-da.]

작년에 비해 공휴일이 삼 일 많습니다.
[jak-nyeon-e bi-hae gong-hyu-il-i sam il man-seup-ni-da.]

한국의 공휴일은 비교적 많습니다.
[o wol-e i-teul deo man-a-jyeot-seup-ni-da.]

그리고, 지하철 요금이 삼백원 올랐습니다.
[geu-ri-go, ji-ha-cheol yo-geum-i sam-baek-won ol-lat-seup-ni-da.]

사년만에 처음 올랐습니다.
[sa-nyeon-man-e cheo-eum ol-lat-seup-ni-da.]

지하철 보다, 버스를 이용하는 사람이 많습니다.
[ji-ha-cheol bo-da, beo-seu-reul i-yong-ha-neun sa-ram-i man-seup-ni-da.]

버스 요금은 지하철보다 낮습니다.
[beo-seu yo-geum-eun ji-ha-cheol-bo-da nat-seup-ni-da.]

버스는 저녁 열두시가 되면 운행이 끝납니다.
[beo-seu-neun jeo-nyeok yeol-du-shi-ga doe-myeon un-haeng-i kkeut-nap-ni-da.]

택시는 언제나 이용 할 수 있습니다.
[taek-shi-neun eon-je-na i-yong hal su it-seup-ni-da.]

학생들은 버스나 지하철을 많이 이용합니다.
[hak-saeng-deul-eun beo-seu-na ji-ha-cheol-eul man-i i-yong-hap-ni-da.]

회사원은 택시를 많이 이용합니다.
[hoe-sa-won-eun taek-shi-reul man-i i-yong-hap-ni-da.]

한국의 대중교통은 굉장히 편리합니다.
[han-guk-eui dae-jung-gyo-tong-eun goeng-jang-hi pyeon-ri-hap-ni-da .]

Question 1. According to the passage, when are many changes going to take place?

1. This Year 2. Next Year 3. Next Century 4. Next Month 5. Next Decade

Question 2. According to the passage, there is more of THIS compared to last year.

1. Holidays 2. Public Schools 3. Drug Stores 4. Restaurants 5. Baseball Stadiums

Question 3. True or False...? There are relatively many holidays in Korea.

1. True 2. False

Question 4. According to the passage, what else changed?

1. Average Age 2. Tuition 3. Text Book Price 4. Insurance Fee 5. Subway Fare

Question 5. According to the passage, it's the first increase in...

1. Three Months 2. Five Months 3. Four Years 4. Ten Years 5. Two Decades

Question 6. True or False...? There are more people taking the bus than the subway.

1. True 2. False

Question 7. True or False...? Bus fare is lower than subway fare.

1. True 2. False

Question 8. According to the passage, the bus service ends at...

1. 10:00 p.m. 2. 11:00 p.m. 3. 0:00 a.m. 4. 2:00 a.m. 5. 4:00 a.m.

Question 9. True or False...? You can use the taxi service anytime you want.

1. True 2. False

Question 10. True or False...? Students take bicycles the most.

1. True 2. False

Question 11. According to the passage, who takes a taxi a lot?

1. Students 2. Parents 3. Teachers 4. Businessmen 5. Foreigners

Question 12. True or False...? The speaker thinks public transportation in Korea is convenient.

1. True 2. False

Practice #22 (Difficulty ★ ★ ★ ☆ ☆)

Read the following passage carefully and answer the following questions.

저는 요즘 요리를 배우고 있습니다.
[jeon-neun yo-jeun yo-ri-reul bae-u-go it-seup-ni-da.]

취미로 시작했습니다.
[chwi-mi-ro shi-jak-haet-seup-ni-da]

하지만 요리는 매우 복잡합니다.
[ha-ji-man yo-ri-neun mae-u bok-jap-hap-ni-da.]

다양한 재료에 대해서 공부해야 합니다.
[da-yang-han jae-ryo-e dae-hae-seo gong-bu-hae-ya hap-ni-da.]

그리고, 신선한 재료를 써야합니다.
[geu-ri-go, shin-seon-han jae-ryo-reul sseo-ya-hap-ni-da]

개인적으로 좋아하는 요리는 한식입니다.
[gae-in-jeok-eu-ro jo-a-ha-neun yo-ri-neun han-shik-ip-ni-da.]

그 중에서도 고기 요리를 좋아합니다.
[geu jung-e-seo-do go-gi yo-ri-reul jo-a-hap-ni-da.]

소고기 보다는 돼지고기가 지방이 적습니다.
[so-go-gi bo-da-neun doe-ji-go-gi-ga ji-bang-i jeok-seup-ni-da.]

지방이 적으면, 살이 찌지 않습니다.
[ji-bang-i jeok-eu-myeon, sal-i jji-ji an-seup-ni-da.]

제가 생각하는 좋은 요리는, 영양이 풍부한 것 입니다.
[je-ga saeng-gak-ha-neun jo-eun yo-ri-neun, yeong-yang-i pung-bu-han geo-ship-ni-da.]

맛 보다, 영양이 더 중요합니다.
[mat bo-da, yeong-yang-i deo jung-yo-hap-ni-da.]

비싸다고 좋은 요리는 아닙니다.
[bi-ssa-da-go jo-eun yo-ri-neun a-nip-ni-da.]

Question 1. According to the passage, what is the speaker learning?

1. Cooking 2. Foreign Language 3. Swimming 4. Golf 5. Singing

Question 2. According to the passage, the speaker started it as a...

1. Rehab Program 2. Hobby 3. Full-Time Job 4. Part-Time Job 5. Study

Question 3. True or False...? According to the speaker, it is simpler than you think.

1. True 2. False

Question 4. According to the passage, what do you have to study?

1. Consumer Behavior 2. Market Trend 3. Flavor Combination 4. Various Ingredients 5. History

Question 5. According to the passage, you have to use...

1. Fresh Ingredients 2. Expensive Silverware 3. Fancy Dishes 4. Clean Tablecloth 5. Natural Furniture

Question 6. According to the passage, the speaker personally likes THIS.

1. Japanese Food 2. Fast Food 3. Chinese Food 4. Korean Food 5. Porridge

Question 7. True or False...? The speaker is a vegetarian.

1. True 2. False

Question 8. True or False...? Pork has more fat than beef.

1. True 2. False

Question 9. According to the passage, less fat helps you...

1. Not Get Fat 2. Have a Balanced Body 3. Eat Less 4. Sleep Better 5. Study More

Question 10. According to the passage, the speaker thinks that a good meal is something that is...

1. Traditional 2. Inexpensive 3. Fresh and Natural 4. Rich in Nutrition 5. Loved by People of All Ages

Question 11. True or False...? The speaker thinks flavor is more important than nutrition.

1. True 2. False

Question 12. True or False...? The speaker thinks good meals are always expensive.

1. True 2. False

Read the following passage carefully and answer the following questions.

오늘은 동물원으로 소풍을 다녀왔습니다.
[o-neul-eun dong-mul-won-eu-ro so-pung-eul da-nyeo-wat-seup-ni-da.]

관람객이 평소보다 많았습니다.
[gwan-ram-gaek-i pyeong-so-bo-da man-at-seup-ni-da.]

날씨가 따뜻했기 때문입니다.
[nal-ssi-ga tta-tteut-haet-gi ttae-mun-ip-ni-da.]

많은 학생들이 구경을 왔습니다.
[man-eun hak-saeng-deul-i gu-gyeong-eul wat-seup-ni-da.]

도시에는 동물이 많이 없어서입니다.
[do-shi-e-neun dong-mul-i man-i eop-seo-seo-ip-ni-da.]

가장 인기가 많은 동물은 원숭이입니다.
[ga-jang in-gi-ga man-eun dong-mul-eun won-sung-i-ip-ni-da.]

사람과 닮아서 그렇습니다.
[sa-ram-gwa dal-ma-seo geu-reot-seup-ni-da.]

하지만 저는 기분이 좋지 않았습니다.
[ha-ji-man jeo-neun gi-bun-i jot-chi an-at-seup-ni-da.]

동물들이 자유롭지 못해 보였기 때문입니다.
[dong-mul-deul-i ja-yu-rop-ji mot-hae bo-yeot-gi ttae-mun-ip-ni-da.]

동물들은 좁은 공간에서 살고 있었습니다.
[dong-mul-deul-eun job-eun gong-gan-e-seo sal-go it-seot-sseup-ni-da.]

그래서, 저는 수의사가 되기로 결정했습니다.
[geu-rae-seo, jeo-neun su-ui-sa-ga doe-gi-ro gyeol-jeong-haet-seup-ni-da.]

아픈 동물들을 치료해주고 싶어서입니다.
[a-peun dong-mul-deul-eul chi-ryo-hae-ju-go ship-eo-seo ip-ni-da.]

Question 1. According to the passage, where did the speaker go to on a picnic?

1. Library 2. National Park 3. The Zoo 4. The Beach 5. Baseball Game

Question 2. True or False...? There were fewer people than usual.

1. True 2. False

Question 3. According to the passage, it was because...

1. The Weather Was Warm 2. A Holiday 3. Admission Was Free 4. The Subway Broke Down

Question 4. According to the passage, many of THIS group of spectators came to visit.

1. Students 2. Children 3. Teachers 4. Parents 5. Foreigners

Question 5. According to the passage, they visited because...

1. It's Their Only Off Day 2. There Aren't Many Animals in The City 3. They Had No Homework
4. They Wanted To Learn Korean Culture 5. They Had To Write a Report

Question 6. According to the passage, the most popular animal is...

1. Monkey 2. Lion 3. Parrot 4. Tiger 5. Polar Bear

Question 7. True or False...? It's because they can do a lot of tricks.

1. True 2. False

Question 8. True or False...? The speaker felt excited to see the animals.

1. True 2. False

Question 9. According to the passage, why did the speaker feel that way?

1. Animals Are Scary 2. Animals Didn't Look Happy 3. Animals Didn't Look Free 4. Animals Were
Obese 5. Animals Looked Healthy

Question 10. According to the passage, animals live in...

1. Small Space 2. Large Cage 3. Dangerous Environment 4. Monitored Settings 5. Underground

Question 11. According to the passage, the speaker decided to become a...

1. Professor 2. Police Officer 3. Ambassador 4. Animal Advocate 5. Veterinarian

Question 12. According to the passage, the speaker wants to...

1. Treat Sick Animals 2. Comfort Lost Animals 3. Adopt Abandoned Animals
4. Start a Charity Foundation 5. Free Captured Animals

Read the following passage carefully and answer the following questions.

작년에는 한국에 약 오백만 명의 관광객이 왔습니다.
[jak-nyeon-e-neun han-guk-e yak o-baek-man myeong-ui gwan-gwang-gaek-i wat-seup-ni-da.]

일본에서 가장 많이 왔습니다.
[il-bon-e-seo ga-jang man-i wat-seup-ni-da.]

일본은 가까운 나라입니다.
[il-bon-eun ga-kka-un na-ra-ip-ni-da.]

문화적으로도 비슷한 점이 많습니다.
[mun-hwa-jeok-eu-ro-do bi-seut-han jeom-i man-seup-ni-da.]

일본 관광객은 한국 화장품을 많이 삽니다.
[il-bon gwan-gwang-gaek-eun han-guk-hwa-jang-pum-eul man-i sap-ni-da.]

중국 관광객은 인삼을 많이 삽니다.
[jung-guk gwan-gwang-gaek-eun in-sam-eul man-i sap-ni-da.]

미국 관광객은 박물관에 많이 갑니다.
[mi-guk gwan-gwang-gaek-eun bak-mul-gwan-e man-i gap-ni-da.]

저는 영어 통역사로 봉사활동을 합니다..
[jeo-neun yeong-eo tong-yeok-sa-ro bong-sa-hwal-dong-eul hap-ni-da.]

한국의 문화에 대해 설명합니다.
[han-guk-ui mun-hwa-e dae-hae seol-myeong-hap-ni-da.]

저도 새롭게 배우는 것이 많습니다.
[jeo-do sae-rop-ge bae-u-neun geo-shi man-seup-ni-da.]

외국인들이 가장 궁금해 하는 것은 한국의 미래입니다.
[oe-guk-in-deul-i ga-jang gung-geum-hae ha-neun geo-seun han-guk-ui mi-rae-ip-ni-da.]

통일이 언제 될지를 가장 많이 물어봅니다.
[tong-il-i eon-je doel-ji-reul ga-jang man-i mul-eo-bop-ni-da.]

Question 1. According to the passage, about how many tourists visited Seoul last year?

1. One Million 2. Two Million 3. Three Million 4. Four Million 5. Five Million

Question 2. According to the passage, the largest number of tourists came from THIS country.

1. Russia 2. U.S.A 3. Canada 4. China 5. Japan

Question 3. True or False...? Japan is quite far from Korea.

1. True 2. False

Question 4. True or False...? Japan has a culture that's drastically different from Korea.

1. True 2. False

Question 5. According to the passage, Japanese tourists buy lots of THIS.

1. Korean Snacks 2. Korean Cosmetics 3. Korean Postcards 4. Korean Clothes 5. Korean Toys

Question 6. According to the passage, Chinese tourists buy lots of THIS.

1. Ginseng 2. Cosmetics 3. Liquor 4. Clothes 5. Books

Question 7. According to the passage, American tourists visit THIS place a lot.

1. Art Gallery 2. Museum 3. Baseball Stadium 4. Korean War Memorial 5. Folk Village

Question 8. According to the passage, the speaker volunteers as a...

1. Tour Guide 2. English Interpreter 3. Security Guard 4. Receptionist 5. Korean Teacher

Question 9. According to the passage, the speaker explains to the tourists about...

1. Korean Language 2. Korean History 3. Korean Culture 4. Korean Art 5. Korean Food

Question 10. True or False...? The speaker knows everything about Korean culture.

1. True 2. False

Question 11. According to the passage, foreigners are most curious about...

1. The History of Korea 2. The Future of Korea 3. The Technology of Korea 4. The Language of Korea
5. The Relationship With Other Countries

Question 12. According to the passage, they ask about THIS the most.

1. When Korea Will Be Unified 2. When Korea Was Divided 3. What Language Koreans Speak
4. Who Lives In Korea 5. What Koreans Do For a Living

Read the following passage carefully and answer the following questions.

서울의 대중교통은 매우 편리합니다.
[seo-ul-ui dae-jung-gyo-tong-eun mae-u pyeon-ri-hap-ni-da.]

외국인들도 쉽게 사용 할 수 있습니다.
[oe-guk-in-deul-do ship-ge sa-yong hal su it-seup-ni-da.]

버스는 때때로 예정된 시간보다 늦게 도착합니다.
[beo-seu-neun ttae-ttae-ro ye-jeong-doen shi-gan-bo-da neut-ge do-chak-hap-ni-da.]

하지만 지하철은 정확합니다.
[ha-ji-man ji-ha-cheol-eun jeong-hwak-hap-ni-da.]

중요한 모임이 있으면, 지하철을 추천합니다.
[jung-yo-han mo-im-i it-seu-myeon, ji-ha-cheol-eul chu-cheon-hap-ni-da.]

지하철을 탈때 가장 어려운 것은 환승입니다.
[je-ha-cheol-eul tal-ttae ga-jang eo-ryeo-un geo-seun hwan-seung-ip-ni-da.]

하지만 안내방송을 들으면 문제가 없습니다.
[ha-ji-man an-nae-bang-song-eul deul-eu-myeon mun-je-ga eop-seup-ni-da.]

여러 나라의 언어로 방송을 합니다.
[yeo-reo na-ra-ui eon-eo-ro bang-song-eul hap-ni-da.]

버스를 타면, 밖을 볼 수 있어 좋습니다.
[beo-seu-reul ta-myeon, bak-eul bol su it-seo jot-seup-ni-da.]

저녁에는 서울의 야경도 볼 수 있습니다.
[jeo-nyeok-e-neun seo-ul-ui ya-gyeong-do bol su it-seup-ni-da.]

그 중에서도 한강을 추천합니다.
[geu jung-e-seo-do han-gang-eul chu-cheon-hap-ni-da.]

서울은 아름답고 낭만적인 곳입니다.
[a-reum-dap-go nang-man-jeok-in got-ip-ni-da.]

Question 1. True or False...? Public transportation in Seoul is not well developed.

1. True 2. False

Question 2. True or False...? Foreigners will have a hard time using Seoul's public transportation.

1. True 2. False

Question 3. True or False...? Korean buses always arrive on time.

1. True 2. False

Question 4. True or False...? Subway often misses scheduled time.

1. True 2. False

Question 5. According to the passage, it's better to take THIS if you have an important meeting.

1. Airplane 2. Taxi 3. Bus 4. Subway 5. Bicycle

Question 6. According to the passage, the most difficult part of taking the subway is...

1. Transfer 2. Buying Ticket 3. Charging Subway Card 4. Security 5. Language Barrier

Question 7. According to the passage, you won't have a problem if you do THIS...

1. Listen To Announcements 2. Bring a Map 3. Bring Cash 4. Take Pictures 5. Ask People

Question 8. True or False...? Announcements are provided in Korean and English.

1. True 2. False

Question 9. According to the passage, what's the good part of taking a bus?

1. You Can Look Outside 2. It's Cheaper 3. It's Safer 4. It's Faster 5. It's Less Crowded

Question 10. True or False...? You can't enjoy Seoul's night view from a bus.

1. True 2. False

Question 11. According to the passage, the speaker recommends...

1. Namsan Tower 2. Han River 3. Seokchon Lake 4. Lotte World 5. DMZ

Question 12. According to the passage, what kind of place in Seoul?

1. Dangerous 2. Scary 3. Safe 4. Inspiring 5. Beautiful and Romantic

Practice #26 (Difficulty ★ ★ ★ ☆ ☆)

Read the following passage carefully and answer the following questions.

한글날은 한글이 만들어진 날입니다.
[han-geul-nal-eun han-geul-i man-deul-eo-jin nal-ip-ni-da.]

세종대왕이 만들었습니다.
[se-jong-dae-wang-i man-deul-eot-seup-ni-da.]

한글이 없었을 때에는, 중국의 문자를 사용했습니다.
[han-geul-i eop-seot-seul ttae-e-neun, jung-guk-ui mun-ja-reul sa-yong-haet-seup-ni-da.]

하지만, 가난한 사람들은 배울 수 없었습니다.
[ha-ji-man, ga-nan-han sa-ram-deul-eun bae-ul su eop-seot-seup-ni-da.]

그래서, 글을 읽을 수 없는 사람이 많았습니다.
[geu-rae-seo, geul-eul il-geul su eop-neun sa-ram-i man-at-seup-ni-da.]

한글은 자음과 모음으로 구성되어 있습니다.
[han-geul-eun ja-eum-gwa mo-eum-eu-ro gu-seong-doe-eo it-seup-ni-da.]

규칙을 알면, 배우기가 아주 쉽습니다.
[gyu-chik-eul al-myeon, bae-u-gi-ga a-ju ship-seup-ni-da.]

외국인들도 한 시간이면 배울 수 있습니다.
[oe-guk-in-deul-do han shi-gan-i-myeon bae-ul su it-seup-ni-da.]

한국인 거의 모두, 한글을 읽을 수 있습니다.
[han-guk-in geo-ui mo-du, han-geul-eul il-geul su it-seup-ni-da.]

한국어는 어렵지만, 한글은 쉽습니다.
[han-guk-eo-neun eo-ryeop-ji-man, han-geul-eun ship-seup-ni-da.]

쓰기와 읽기를 연습하면 도움이 됩니다.
[sseu-gi-wa il-gi-reul yeon-seup-ma-myeon, do-um-i doep-ni-da.]

한글은 한국 문화의 자랑입니다.
[han-geul-eun han-guk mun-hwa-ui ja-rang-ip-ni-da.]

Question 1. True or False...? 한글날 is the day the Korean alphabet was made.

1. True 2. False

Question 2. According to the passage, who made Hangeul?

1. King Gojong 2. King Sejong 3. Queen Gwang 4. Professor Lee 5. Chinese Scholars

Question 3. True or False...? Koreans used Japanese characters before Hangeul was made.

1. True 2. False

Question 4. According to the passage, who could not learn it?

1. Rich People 2. Poor People 3. Disabled People 4. Women 5. Blind People

Question 5. True or False...? Despite the problem mentioned above, many people were able to read.

1. True 2. False

Question 6. According to the passage, Hangeul is made up of...

1. Consonants Only 2. Consonants and Syllables 3. Consonants and Vowels 4. Vowels Only 5. Symbols

Question 7. According to the passage, it's easy to learn Hangeul once you know the...

1. History 2. Rules 3. Shapes 4. Dynamics 5. Names

Question 8. According to the passage, foreigners can learn Hangeul in...

1. An Hour 2. Two Days 3. Three Weeks 4. A Month 5. A Year

Question 9. True or False...? About half of the Korean population can read.

1. True 2. False

Question 10. True or False...? Korean language and Hangeul are both difficult to learn.

1. True 2. False

Question 11. According to the passage, what can help you learn Hangeul?

1. Reading and Listening 2. Writing and Singing 3. Reading Only 4. Reading and Writing 5. Writing and Memorizing

Question 12. According to the passage, Hangeul is the pride of Korean...

1. History 2. Art 3. Science 4. Education 5. Culture

Practice #27 (Difficulty ★ ★ ★ ☆ ☆)

Read the following passage carefully and answer the following questions.

한복은 한국인의 전통 의상입니다.
[han-bok-eun han-guk-in-ui jeon-tong ui-sang-ip-ni-da.]

언제부터 입었는지는 정확히 모릅니다.
[eon-je-bu-teo ip-eot-neun-ji-neun jeong-hwak-hi mo-reup-ni-da.]

기록이 없기 때문입니다.
[gi-rok-i eop-gi ttae-mun-ip-ni-da.]

한복의 매력은 다양한 색상입니다.
[han-bok-ui mae-ryeok-eun da-yang-han saek-sang-ip-ni-da.]

분홍, 파랑, 하양, 노랑이 가장 많이 쓰입니다.
[bun-hong, pa-rang, ha-yang, no-rang-i ga-jang man-i sseu-ip-ni-da.]

하지만 요즘에는 한복을 많이 입지 않습니다.
[ha-ji-man yo-jeum-e-neun han-bok-eul man-i ip-ji an-seup-ni-da.]

입기에 불편하기 때문입니다.
[ip-gi-e bul-pyeon-ha-gi ttae-mun-ip-ni-da.]

전통 명절에만 입습니다.
[jeon-tong myeong-jeol-e-man.ip-seup-ni-da.]

그래서, 새로운 한복을 만드는 사람들이 있습니다.
[geu-rae-seo, sae-ro-un han-bok-eul man-deu-neun sa-ram-deul-i it-seup-ni-da.]

더욱 단순한 디자인을 사용합니다.
[deo-uk dan-sun-han di-ja-in-eul sa-yong-hap-ni-da.]

젊은 사람들에게 인기가 많습니다.
[jeol-meun sa-ram-deul-e-ge in-gi-ga man-seup-ni-da.]

다시 한복의 인기가 많아질 것으로 기대됩니다.
[da-shi han-bok-ui in-gi-ga man-a-jil geot-eu-ro gi-dae-doep-ni-da.]

Question 1. According to the passage, what is the name of Korean traditional clothes?

1. Hanguk 2. Hanbok 3. Jeon Tong 4. Ui Sang 5. In Ui

Question 2. True or False...? It has been worn since Gojoseon period.

1. True 2. False

Question 3. True or False...? There is a detailed historical record of the traditional clothes.

1. True 2. False

Question 4. According to the passage, what is the beauty of Korean traditional clothes?

1. Sophisticated Designs 2. Various Colors 3. Long History 4. Famous Designers 5. Durability

Question 5. According to the passage, which of the following colors is not frequently used?

1. Black 2. Pink 3. Blue 4. White 5. Yellow

Question 6. True or False...? More people are wearing it than ever before.

1. True 2. False

Question 7. According to the passage, the reason for the above is because it's...

1. Comfortable To Wear 2. Uncomfortable To Wear 3. Expensive To Buy 4. Unattractive 5. Outdated

Question 8. According to the passage, when is it worn?

1. Only On Weekend 2. Only On Traditional Holidays 3. Whenever Possible 4. During The Winter
5. In The Afternoon

Question 9. According to the passage, there are people who are...

1. Making New Hanbok 2. Rebranding Hanbok 3. Outsourcing Hanbok 4. Boycotting Hanbok
5. Promoting Hanbok

Question 10. According to the passage, what do the people mentioned above use?

1. Simpler Design 2. More Sophisticated Design 3. More Affordable Materials
4. More Modern Elements 5. More Colorful Design

Question 11. True or False...? Such clothes mentioned above are popular among...

1. Children 2. Young People 3. Professors 4. Parents 5. Senior Citizens

Question 12. According to the passage, the speaker expects that Hanbok will be...

1. Less Popular Than Before 2. Popular Again 3. Abandoned 4. More Expensive 5. More Comfortable

Read the following passage carefully and answer the following questions.

한국에는 재밌는 미신들이 있습니다.
[han-guk-e-neun jae-mit-neun mi-shin-deul-i it-seup-ni-da.]

동물에 관한 것들이 많습니다.
[dong-mul-e gwan-han geot-deul-i man-seup-ni-da.]

돼지 꿈을 꾸면, 행운이 온다는 것입니다.
[doe-ji kkum-eul kku-myeon, haeng-un-i on-da-neun geo-ship-ni-da.]

돼지는 돈을 상징하기 때문입니다.
[doe-ji-neun don-eul sang-jing-ha-gi ttae-mun-ip-ni-da.]

그래서 사람들은 돼지 꿈을 꾸면, 복권을 삽니다.
[geu-rae-seo sa-ram-deul-eun doe-ji kkum-eul kku-myeon, bok-gwon-eul sap-ni-da.]

까치에 관한 미신도 있습니다.
[kka-chi-e gwan-han mi-shin-do it-seup-ni-da.]

까치가 울면, 손님이 온다고 합니다.
[kka-chi-ga ul-myeon, son-nim-i on-da-go hap-ni-da.]

미신은 과학적인 근거는 없습니다.
[mi-shin-eun gwa-hak-jeok-in geun-geo-neun eop-seup-ni-da.]

하지만, 많은 사람들이 믿고 즐깁니다.
[ha-ji-man, man-eun sa-ram-deul-i mit-go jeul-gip-ni-da.]

미신은 문화와 관계가 있습니다.
[mi-shin-eun mun-hwa-wa gwan-gye-ga it-seup-ni-da.]

문화가 비슷하면, 미신도 비슷합니다.
[mun-hwa-ga bi-seut-ha-myeon, mi-shin-do bi-seut-hap-ni-da.]

그래서 일본과 중국에도 비슷한 미신이 있습니다.
[geu-rae-seo il-bon-gwa jung-guk-e-do bi-seut-han mi-shin-i it-seup-ni-da.]

Question 1. According to the passage, there are many fun (   ) in Korea.

1. Folk Tales 2. Novels 3. Myths 4. Movies 5. Records

Question 2. True or False...? There are many myths about animals

1. True 2. False

Question 3. According to the passage, doing THIS is believed to bring good fortune.

1. Having Pig Dreams 2. Eating Pork 3. Raising a Pig 4. Adopting a Pig 5. Keeping a Piggy Bank

Question 4. According to the passage, the reason for the above is because pigs symbolize...

1. Bad Fortune 2. Money 3. Safety 4. Security 5. Loyalty

Question 5. According to the passage, what do people do after having a "pig dream"?

1. Buy a New House 2. Open a New Bank Account 3. Buy Lottery Tickets 4. Gamble 5. Sell Belongings

Question 6. The speaker introduces another myth about a...

1. Magpie 2. Blue Bird 3. Puppy 4. Rabbit 5. Tiger

Question 7. According to the passage, if the above-mentioned animal cries, it means...

1. Guest Will Come 2. Bad News Is Coming 3. Good Fortune Is coming 4. You Will Get Healthy
5. You Will Lose Money

Question 8. True or False...? Myths are based on science.

1. True 2. False

Question 9. True or False...? Many people believe and enjoy them.

1. True 2. False

Question 10. According to the passage, myths are related to...

1. Art 2. Culture 3. History 4. Language 5. Food

Question 11. True or False...? If cultures are similar, myths are also similar.

1. True 2. False

Question 12. According to the passage, similar myths are found in...

1. Japan and Vietnam 2. China and North Korea 3. North Korea and South Korea 4. Japan and China

Read the following passage carefully and answer the following questions.

저희 동네 도서관에는 희귀한 책이 많습니다.
[jeo-hui dong-ne do-seo-gwan-e-neun hui-gwi-han chaek-i man-seup-ni-da.]

천 년 전에 만들어진 책도 있습니다.
[cheon nyeon jeon-e man-deul-eo-jin chaek-do it-seup-ni-da.]

이러한 책들은 특별한 곳에 보관합니다.
[i-reo-han chaek-deul-eun teuk-byeol-han go-se bo-gwan-hap-ni-da.]

직원들만 들어갈 수 있는 곳입니다.
[jik-won-deul-man deul-eo-gal su it-neun go-ship-ni-da.]

하지만 가끔씩 일반인에게도 공개가 됩니다.
[ha-ji-man ga-ggeum-ssik il-ban-in-e-ge-do gong-gae-ga doep-ni-da.]

일년에 한 번, 특별한 행사가 있습니다.
[il-nyeon-e han beon, teuk-byeol-han haeng-sa-ga it-seup-ni-da.]

아쉽지만, 사진을 찍을 수 는 없습니다.
[a-ship-ji-man, sa-jin-eul jjik-eul su neun eop-seup-ni-da.]

저도 행사에 가 본 적이 있습니다.
[jeo-do haeng-sa-e ga bon jeok-i it-seup-ni-da.]

그 날에는, 다른 나라에서도 손님이 많이 옵니다.
[geu nal-e-neun, da-reun na-ra-e-seo-do son-nim-i man-i op-ni-da.]

줄이 너무 길어서 한참을 기다렸습니다.
[jul-i neo-mu gil-eo-seo han-cham-eul gi-da-ryeot-seup-ni-da.]

그래도, 그럴만한 가치가 있었습니다.
[geu-rae-do, geu-reol-man-han ga-chi-ga it-seot-seup-ni-da.]

다음 행사는 내년 봄에 있습니다.
[da-eum haeng-sa-neun nae-nyeon bom-e it-seup-ni-da.]

Question 1. According to the passage, the library in the speaker's town has a lot of...

1. Old Books 2. Rare Books 3. Expensive Books 4. Fake Books 5. Original Books

Question 2. True or False...? The library even has a book that's one thousand years old.

1. True 2. False

Question 3. According to the passage, such books are kept in...

1. Secret Chamber 2. Special Place 3. Digital Archive 4. Central Library 5. Government Facility

Question 4. According to the passage, who can enter such a place mentioned above?

1. Professors 2. Government Officials 3. Scholars 4. Employees 5. Paying Guests

Question 5. True or False...? Such books are never shown to the general public.

1. True 2. False

Question 6. According to the passage, how often is there a special event?

1. Every Weekend 2. Every Month 3. Once A Year 4. Once Every Two Years 5. Once Every Decade

Question 7. True or False...? You are free to take photos on that day.

1. True 2. False

Question 8. According to the passage, the speaker had never been to such an event.

1. True 2. False

Question 9. True or False...? People from other countries are not allowed to visit such an event.

1. True 2. False

Question 10. According to the passage, the speaker had to wait for a long time because...

1. The Line Was Too Long 2. The Weather Was Too Bad 3. Library Wasn't Ready
4. Theft Took Place 5. Books Were Damaged

Question 11. True or False...? The speaker thinks it was worth the wait.

1. True 2. False

Question 12. According to the passage, when is the next event?

1. This Winter 2. Next Summer 3. Next Winter 4. Next Spring 5. In Two Years

Read the following passage carefully and answer the following questions.

자동차는 만 개 이상의 부품으로 만들어집니다.
[ja-dong-cha-neun man gae i-sang-ui bu-pum-eu-ro man-deul-eo-jip-ni-da.]

대부분 자동으로 조립됩니다.
[dae-bu-bun ja-dong-eu-ro jo-rip-doep-ni-da.]

자동차를 만드는 것은 시간이 많이 걸리지 않습니다.
[ja-dong-cha-reul man-deu-neun geo-seun shi-gan-i man-i geol-li-ji an-seup-ni-da.]

예전에는 한 달 정도 걸렸습니다.
[ye-jeon-e-neun han dal jeong-do geol-ryeot-seup-ni-da.]

모두 사람이 만들어야 했기 때문입니다.
[mo-du sa-ram-i man-deul-eo-ya haet-gi ttae-mun-ip-ni-da.]

지금은 약 백분의 일 정도 시간이 걸립니다.
[ji-geum-eun yak baek-bun-ui il jeong-do shi-gan-i geol-lip-ni-da.]

기계가 없었으면, 자동차는 매우 비쌌을 겁니다.
[gi-gye-ga eop-seot-seu-myeon, ja-dong-cha-neun mae-u bi-ssat-seul geop-ni-da.]

그리고, 자전거를 타는 사람이 더 많았을 겁니다.
[geu-ri-go, ja-jeon-geo-reul ta-neun sa-ram-i deo man-at-seul geop-ni-da]

물론, 자전거를 타는 것은 건강에 더 좋습니다.
[mul-lon, ja-jeon-geo-reul ta-neun geo-seun geon-gang-e deo jot-seup-ni-da.]

하지만, 멀리 가기에는 힘이 듭니다.
[ha-ji-man, meol-li ga-gi-e-neun him-i deup-ni-da.]

자동차는 우리의 생활을 편하게 해줍니다.
[ja-dong-cha-neun u-ri-ui saeng-hwal-eul pyeon-ha-ge hae-jup-ni-da.]

하지만, 술을 마시고 운전하면 위험합니다
[ha-ji-man, sul-eul ma-shi-go un-jeon-ha-myeon wi-heom-hap-ni-da.]

Question 1. True or False...? Cars are made of less than five thousand parts.

1. True 2. False

Question 2. True or False...? Most of the parts are put together by human hands.

1. True 2. False

Question 3. True or False...? Making cars doesn't take much time.

1. True 2. False

Question 4. According to the passage, how much time did it take to make a car in the past?

1. About A Day 2. About A Week 3. About A Month 4. About Two Months 5. About A Year

Question 5. According to the passage, the main reason for taking so much time is because...

1. Only Men Could Work 2. Only Experts Could Do The Job 3. Everything Had To Be Done By Human 4. People Were Less Skillful 5. Work Hours Were Shorter

Question 6. Compared to the past, how much time does it take now?

1. 1/10 2. 1/100 3. 1/1000 4. Double 5. Triple

Question 7. According to the passage, cars would have been very expensive if there were no...

1. Machines 2. Technology 3. Labor Union 4. Gasoline 5. Factories

Question 8. According to the passage, there could have been more of THIS as a result of the above.

1. People Who Ride Bicycles 2. People Who Walk 3. Buses 4. Telephones 5. Elevators

Question 9. According to the passage, the benefit of riding a bicycle is that it's better for...

1. Fuel Efficiency 2. The Environment 3. Health 4. Muscles 5. The Economy

Question 10. According to the passage, the downside of riding a bicycle is that it's difficult to...

1. Go Continuously 2. Go Far 3. Stop Once You're On The Road 4. Go Fast 5. Change Speeds

Question 11. True or False...? According to the speaker, cars make our lives...

1. More Complicated 2. More Dangerous 3. Less Dangerous 4. More Convenient 5. Time Efficient

Question 12. According to the passage, what is a dangerous act?

1. Driving With Eyes Closed 2. Driving While Sleepy 3. Driving After Drinking 4. Driving Without License 5. Driving Without Insurance

Practice #21

올 해 부터는 많은 것들이 달라집니다.
Lots of things will change starting this year.
[ol hae bu-teo-neun man-eun geot-deul-i dal-la-jip-ni-da.]
작년에 비해 공휴일이 삼 일 많습니다.
Compare to last year, there are three more public holidays.
[jak-nyeon-e bi-hae gong-hyu-il-i sam il man-seup-ni-da.]
한국의 공휴일은 비교적 많습니다.
Relatively, there are many public holidays in Korea.
[o wol-e i-teul deo man-a-jyeot-seup-ni-da.]
그리고, 지하철 요금이 삼백원 올랐습니다.
And, the subway fare has increased by three hundred won.
[geu-ri-go, ji-ha-cheol yo-geum-i sam-baek-won ol-lat-seup-ni-da.]
사년만에 처음 올랐습니다.
It's the first increase in four years.
[sa-nyeon-man-e cheo-eum ol-lat-seup-ni-da.]
지하철 보다, 버스를 이용하는 사람이 많습니다.
There are more people using the bus than the subway.
[ji-ha-cheol bo-da, beo-seu-reul i-yong-ha-neun sa-ram-i man-seup-ni-da.]
버스 요금은 지하철보다 낮습니다.
Bus fare is lower than the subway.
[beo-seu yo-geum-eun ji-ha-cheol-bo-da nat-seup-ni-da.]
버스는 저녁 열두시가 되면 운행이 끝납니다.
Bus service ends at twelve at night.
[beo-seu-neun jeo-nyeok yeol-du-shi-ga doe-myeon un-haeng-i kkeut-nap-ni-da.]
택시는 언제나 이용 할 수 있습니다.
You can use a taxi anytime.
[taek-shi-neun eon-je-na i-yong hal su it-seup-ni-da.]
학생들은 버스나 지하철을 많이 이용합니다.
Students use the bus or subway more.
[hak-saeng-deul-eun beo-seu-na ji-ha-cheol-eul man-i i-yong-hap-ni-da.]
회사원은 택시를 많이 이용합니다.
Office workers use taxis more.
[hoe-sa-won-eun taek-shi-reul man-i i-yong-hap-ni-da.]
한국의 대중교통은 굉장히 편리합니다.
Public transportation in Korea is very convenient.
[han-guk-eui dae-jung-gyo-tong-eun goeng-jang-hi pyeon-ri-hap-ni-da.]

Answer Keys : (1) 1 (2) 1 (3) 1 (4) 5 (5) 3 (6) 1 (7) 1 (8) 3
(9) 1 (10) 2 (11) 4 (12) 1

Practice #22

저는 요즘 요리를 배우고 있습니다.
I'm learning cooking these days.
[jeon-neun yo-jeun yo-ri-reul bae-u-go it-seup-ni-da.]
취미로 시작했습니다.
I started it as a hobby.
[chwi-mi-ro shi-jak-haet-seup-ni-da]
하지만 요리는 매우 복잡합니다.
But cooking is very complicated.
[ha-ji-man yo-ri-neun mae-u bok-jap-hap-ni-da.]
다양한 재료에 대해서 공부해야 합니다.
You have to study various ingredients.
[da-yang-han jae-ryo-e dae-hae-seo gong-bu-hae-ya hap-ni-da.]
그리고, 신선한 재료를 써야합니다.
And, you need to use fresh ingredients.
[geu-ri-go, shin-seon-han jae-ryo-reul sseo-ya-hap-ni-da]
개인적으로 좋아하는 요리는 한식입니다.
The food I personally like is Korean food.
[gae-in-jeok-eu-ro jo-a-ha-neun yo-ri-neun han-shik-ip-ni-da.]
그 중에서도 고기 요리를 좋아합니다.
Among all, I like meat dishes.
[geu jung-e-seo-do go-gi yo-ri-reul jo-a-hap-ni-da.]
소고기 보다는 돼지고기가 기름이 적습니다.
Pork has less fat than beef.
[so-go-gi bo-da-neun doe-ji-go-gi-ga gi-reum-i jeok-seup-ni-da.]
기름이 적으면, 살이 찌지 않습니다.
If there's less fat, you don't get fat.
[gi-reum-i jeok-eu-myeon, sal-i jji-ji an-seup-ni-da.]
제가 생각하는 좋은 요리는, 영양이 풍부한 것 입니다.
The good food which I think is rich in nutrition.
[je-ga saeng-gak-ha-neun jo-eun yo-ri-neun, yeong-yang-i pung-bu-han geo-ship-ni-da.]
맛 보다, 영양이 더 중요합니다.
Nutrition is more important than taste.
[mat bo-da, yeong-yang-i deo jung-yo-hap-ni-da.]
비싸다고 좋은 요리는 아닙니다.
It's not necessarily good food just because it's expensive.
[bi-ssa-da-go jo-eun yo-ri-neun a-nip-ni-da.]

Answer Keys : (1) 1 (2) 2 (3) 2 (4) 4 (5) 1 (6) 4 (7) 2 (8) 2
(9) 1 (10) 4 (11) 2 (12) 2

Practice #23

오늘은 동물원으로 소풍을 다녀왔습니다.
Today I came back from a picnic at the zoo.
[o-neul-eun dong-mul-won-eu-ro so-pung-eul da-nyeo-wat-seup-ni-da.]
관람객이 평소보다 많았습니다.
There were more spectators than usual.
[gwan-ram-gaek-i pyeong-so-bo-da man-at-seup-ni-da.]
날씨가 따뜻했기 때문입니다.
It's because the weather was warm.
[nal-ssi-ga tta-tteut-haet-gi ttae-mun-ip-ni-da.]
많은 학생들이 구경을 왔습니다.
Lots of students came to see.
[man-eun hak-saeng-deul-i gu-gyeong-eul wat-seup-ni-da.]
도시에는 동물이 많이 없어서입니다.
It's because there aren't many animals in the city.
[do-shi-e-neun dong-mul-i man-i eop-seo-seo-ip-ni-da.]
가장 인기가 많은 동물은 원숭이입니다.
The most popular animal is the monkeys.
[ga-jang in-gi-ga man-eun dong-mul-eun won-sung-i-ip-ni-da.]
사람과 닮아서 그렇습니다.
It's because they are similar to humans.
[sa-ram-gwa dal-ma-seo geu-reot-seup-ni-da.]
하지만 저는 기분이 좋지 않았습니다.
But I didn't feel good.
[ha-ji-man jeo-neun gi-bun-i jot-chi an-at-seup-ni-da.]
동물들이 자유롭지 못해 보였기 때문입니다.
It's because animals didn't look free.

[dong-mul-deul-i ja-yu-rop-ji mot-hae bo-yeot-gi ttae-mun-ip-ni-da.]
동물들은 좁은 공간에서 살고 있었습니다.
Animals were living in a tight space.
[dong-mul-deul-eun job-eun gong-gan-e-seo sal-go it-seot-sseup-ni-da.]
그래서, 저는 수의사가 되기로 결정했습니다.
So, I decided to become a vet.
[geu-rae-seo, jeo-neun su-ui-sa-ga doe-gi-ro gyeol-jeong-haet-seup-ni-da.]
아픈 동물들을 치료해주고 싶어서입니다.
It's because I want to treat sick animals.
[a-peun dong-mul-deul-eul chi-ryo-hae-ju-go ship-eo-seo ip-ni-da.]

Answer Keys : (1) 3 (2) 2 (3) 1 (4) 1 (5) 2 (6) 1 (7) 2 (8) 2
(9) 3 (10) 1 (11) 5 (12) 1

Practice #24

작년에는 한국에 약 오백만 명의 관광객이 왔습니다.
About five million tourists came to Korea last year.
[jak-nyeon-e-neun han-guk-e yak o-baek-man myeong-ui gwan-gwang-gaek-i wat-seup-ni-da.]
일본에서 가장 많이 왔습니다.
The most came from Japan.
[il-bon-e-seo ga-jang man-i wat-seup-ni-da.]
일본은 가까운 나라입니다.
Japan is a close country.
[il-bon-eun ga-kka-un na-ra-ip-ni-da.]
문화적으로도 비슷한 점이 많습니다.
There are many similarities culturally.
[mun-hwa-jeok-eu-ro-do bi-seut-han jeom-i man-seup-ni-da.]
일본 관광객은 한국 화장품을 많이 삽니다.
Japanese tourists buy lots of Korean cosmetics.
[il-bon gwan-gwang-gaek-eun han-guk-hwa-jang-pum-eul man-i sap-ni-da.]
중국 관광객은 인삼을 많이 삽니다.
Chinese tourists buy lots of ginseng.
[jung-guk gwan-gwang-gaek-eun in-sam-eul man-i sap-ni-da.]
미국 관광객은 박물관에 많이 갑니다.
American tourists go to museums a lot.
[mi-guk gwan-gwang-gaek-eun bak-mul-gwan-e man-i gap-ni-da.]
저는 영어 통역사로 봉사활동을 합니다.
I volunteer as an English interpreter.
[jeo-neun yeong-eo tong-yeok-sa-ro bong-sa-hwal-dong-eul hap-ni-da.]
한국의 문화에 대해 설명합니다.
I explain Korean culture.
[han-guk-ui mun-hwa-e dae-hae seol-myeong-hap-ni-da.]
저도 새롭게 배우는 것이 많습니다.
There are many things that I newly learn.
[jeo-do sae-rop-ge bae-u-neun geo-shi man-seup-ni-da.]
외국인들이 가장 궁금해 하는 것은 한국의 미래입니다.
What foreigners are curious about the most is the future of Korea.
[oe-guk-in-deul-i ga-jang gung-geum-hae ha-neun geo-seun han-guk-ui mi-rae-ip-ni-da.]
통일이 언제 될지를 가장 많이 물어봅니다.

They ask when Korea will be unified the most.
[tong-il-i eon-je doel-ji-reul ga-jang man-i mul-eo-bop-ni-da.]

Answer Keys : (1) 5 (2) 5 (3) 2 (4) 2 (5) 2 (6) 1 (7) 2 (8) 2
(9) 3 (10) 2 (11) 2 (12) 1

Practice #25

서울의 대중교통은 매우 편리합니다.
Public transportation in Seoul is very convenient.
[seo-ul-ui dae-jung-gyo-tong-eun mae-u pyeon-ri-hap-ni-da.]
외국인들도 쉽게 사용 할 수 있습니다.
Foreigners can use it easily.
[oe-guk-in-deul-do ship-ge sa-yong hal su it-seup-ni-da.]
버스는 때때로 예정된 시간보다 늦게 도착합니다.
Buses sometimes arrive later than the scheduled time.
[beo-seu-neun ttae-ttae-ro ye-jeong-doen shi-gan-bo-da neut-ge do-chak-hap-ni-da.]
하지만 지하철은 정확합니다.
But the subway is accurate.
[ha-ji-man ji-ha-cheol-eun jeong-hwak-hap-ni-da.]
중요한 모임이 있으면, 지하철을 추천합니다.
If there is an important meeting, I recommend the subway.
[jung-yo-han mo-im-i it-seu-myeon, ji-ha-cheol-eul chu-cheon-hap-ni-da.]
지하철을 탈때 가장 어려운 것은 환승입니다.
The most difficult thing while taking the subway is transfers.
[je-ha-cheol-eul tal-ttae ga-jang eo-ryeo-un geo-seun hwan-seung-ip-ni-da.]
하지만 안내방송을 들으면 문제가 없습니다.
But if you listen to announcements, there is no problem.
[ha-ji-man an-nae-bang-song-eul deul-eu-myeon mun-je-ga eop-seup-ni-da.]
여러 나라의 언어로 방송을 합니다.
Announcements are made in the languages of many countries.
[yeo-reo na-ra-ui eon-eo-ro bang-song-eul hap-ni-da.]
버스를 타면, 밖을 볼 수 있어 좋습니다.
If you take a bus, it's good because you can see outside.
[beo-seu-reul ta-myeon, bak-eul bol su it-seo jot-seup-ni-da.]
저녁에는 서울의 야경도 볼 수 있습니다.
During the night time, you can see the night view of Seoul
[jeo-nyeok-e-neun seo-ul-ui ya-gyeong-do bol su it-seup-ni-da.]
그 중에서도 한강을 추천합니다.
Among all, I recommend the Han River.
[geu jung-e-seo-do han-gang-eul chu-cheon-hap-ni-da.]
서울은 아름답고 낭만적인 곳입니다.
Seoul is a beautiful and romantic place.
[a-reum-dap-go nang-man-jeok-in got-ip-ni-da.]

Answer Keys : (1) 2 (2) 2 (3) 2 (4) 1 (5) 4 (6) 1 (7) 1 (8) 2
(9) 1 (10) 2 (11) 2 (12) 5

Practice #26

한글날은 한글이 만들어진 날입니다.
Hangeulnal is the day when Hangeul was made.
[han-geul-nal-eun han-geul-i man-deul-eo-jin nal-ip-ni-da.]
세종대왕이 만들었습니다.
King Sejong The Great made it.
[se-jong-dae-wang-i man-deul-eot-seup-ni-da.]
한글이 없었을 때에는, 중국의 문자를 사용했습니

다. When there was no Hangeul, (people) used Chinese characters.
[han-geul-i eop-seot-seul ttae-e-neun, jung-guk-ui mun-ja-reul sa-yong-haet-seup-ni-da.]
하지만, 가난한 사람들은 배울 수 없었습니다.
But poor people couldn't learn it.
[ha-ji-man, ga-nan-han sa-ram-deul-eun bae-ul su eop-seot-seup-ni-da.]
그래서, 글을 읽을 수 없는 사람이 많았습니다.
So, there weren't many people who could read.
[geu-rae-seo, geul-eul il-geul su eop-neun sa-ram-i man-at-seup-ni-da.]
한글은 자음과 모음으로 구성되어 있습니다.
Hangeul is composed of vowels and consonants.
[han-geul-eun ja-eum-gwa mo-eum-eu-ro gu-seong-doe-eo it-seup-ni-da.]
규칙을 알면, 배우기가 아주 쉽습니다.
If you know the patterns, it's very easy to learn.
[gyu-chik-eul al-myeon, bae-u-gi-ga a-ju ship-seup-ni-da.]
외국인들도 한 시간이면 배울 수 있습니다.
Foreginers can learn in an hour.
[oe-guk-in-deul-do han shi-gan-i-myeon bae-ul su it-seup-ni-da.]
한국인 거의 모두, 한글을 읽을 수 있습니다.
Almost every Korean can read Hangeul.
[han-guk-in geo-ui mo-du, han-geul-eul il-geul su it-seup-ni-da.]
한국어는 어렵지만, 한글은 쉽습니다.
The Korean language is difficult, but Hangeul is easy.
[han-guk-eo-neun eo-ryeop-ji-man, han-geul-eun ship-seup-ni-da.]
쓰기와 읽기를 연습하면 도움이 됩니다.
If you practice writing and reading, it's helpful.
[sseu-gi-wa il-gi-reul yeon-seup-ma-myeon, do-um-i doep-ni-da.]
한글은 한국 문화의 자랑입니다.
Hanguel is the pride of Korean culture.
[han-geul-eun han-guk mun-hwa-ui ja-rang-ip-ni-da.]

Answer Keys : (1) 1 (2) 2 (3) 2 (4) 2 (5) 2 (6) 3 (7) 2 (8) 1
(9) 2 (10) 2 (11) 4 (12) 5

Practice #27

한복은 한국인의 전통 의상입니다.
Hanbok is traditional Korean clothes.
[han-bok-eun han-guk-in-ui jeon-tong ui-sang-ip-ni-da.]
언제부터 입었는지는 정확히 모릅니다.
It's not precisely known when it started being worn.
[eon-je-bu-teo ip-eot-neun-ji-neun jeong-hwak-hi mo-reup-ni-da.]
기록이 없기 때문입니다.
It's because there are no records.
[gi-rok-i eop-gi ttae-mun-ip-ni-da.]
한복의 매력은 다양한 색상입니다.
The beauty of Hanbok is various colors.
[han-bok-ui mae-ryeok-eun da-yang-han saek-sang-ip-ni-da.]
분홍, 파랑, 하양, 노랑이 가장 많이 쓰입니다.
Pink, blue, white, and yellow are used the most.
[bun-hong, pa-rang, ha-yang, no-rang-i ga-jang man-i sseu-ip-ni-da.]
하지만 요즘에는 한복을 많이 입지 않습니다.
But Hanbok is not worn a lot these days.
[ha-ji-man yo-jeum-e-neun han-bok-eul man-i ip-ji an-seup-ni-da.]
입기에 불편하기 때문입니다.
It's because it's difficult to wear.
[ip-gi-e bul-pyeon-ha-gi ttae-mun-ip-ni-da.]
전통 명절에만 입습니다.
It's only worn during traditional holidays.
[jeon-tong myeong-jeol-e-man.ip-seup-ni-da.]
그래서, 새로운 한복을 만드는 사람들이 있습니다.
So, there are people who make new Hanbok.
[geu-rae-seo, sae-ro-un han-bok-eul man-deu-neun sa-ram-deul-i it-seup-ni-da.]
더욱 단순한 디자인을 사용합니다.
They use simpler designs.
[deo-uk dan-sun-han di-ja-in-eul sa-yong-hap-ni-da.]
젊은 사람들에게 인기가 많습니다.
It's very popular among the young generation.
[jeol-meun sa-ram-deul-e-ge in-gi-ga man-seup-ni-da.]
다시 한복의 인기가 많아질 것으로 기대됩니다.
It's expected that the popularity of Hanbok will rise again.
[da-shi han-bok-ui in-gi-ga man-a-jil geot-eu-ro gi-dae-doep-ni-da.]

Answer Keys : (1) 2 (2) 2 (3) 2 (4) 2 (5) 1 (6) 2 (7) 2 (8) 2
(9) 1 (10) 1 (11) 2 (12) 2

Practice #28

한국에는 재밌는 미신들이 있습니다.
There are interesting myths in Korea.
[han-guk-e-neun jae-mit-neun mi-shin-deul-i it-seup-ni-da.]
동물에 관한 것들이 많습니다.
There are many about animals.
[dong-mul-e gwan-han geot-deul-i man-seup-ni-da.]
돼지 꿈을 꾸면, 행운이 온다는 것입니다.
It's that if you have a dream of a pig, good fortune will come to you.
[doe-ji kkum-eul kku-myeon, haeng-un-i on-da-neun geo-ship-ni-da.]
돼지는 돈을 상징하기 때문입니다.
It's because pigs symbolize money.
[doe-ji-neun don-eul sang-jing-ha-gi ttae-mun-ip-ni-da.]
그래서 사람들은 돼지 꿈을 꾸면, 복권을 삽니다.
So when people have a dream of a pig, they buy a lottery ticket.
[geu-rae-seo sa-ram-deul-eun doe-ji kkum-eul kku-myeon, bok-gwon-eul sap-ni-da.]
까치에 관한 미신도 있습니다.
There are myths about magpies.
[kka-chi-e gwan-han mi-shin-do it-seup-ni-da.]
까치가 울면, 손님이 온다고 합니다.
It's said that if magpies cry, guests will come.
[kka-chi-ga ul-myeon, son-nim-i on-da-go hap-ni-da.]
미신은 과학적인 근거는 없습니다.
Myths have no scientific base.
[mi-shin-eun gwa-hak-jeok-in geun-geo-neun eop-seup-ni-da.]
하지만, 많은 사람들이 믿고 즐깁니다.
But lots of people believe and enjoy them.

[ha-ji-man, man-eun sa-ram-deul-i mit-go jeul-gip-ni-da.]
미신은 문화와 관계가 있습니다.
Myths are related to culture.
[mi-shin-eun mun-hwa-wa gwan-gye-ga it-seup-ni-da.]
문화가 비슷하면, 미신도 비슷합니다.
If cultures are similar, myths are also similar.
[mun-hwa-ga bi-seut-ha-myeon, mi-shin-do bi-seut-hap-ni-da.]
그래서 일본과 중국에도 비슷한 미신이 있습니다.
So there are similar myths in Japan and China.
[geu-rae-seo il-bon-gwa jung-guk-e-do bi-seut-han mi-shin-i it-seup-ni-da.]

Answer Keys : (1) 3 (2) 1 (3) 1 (4) 2 (5) 3 (6) 1 (7) 1 (8) 2
(9) 1 (10) 2 (11) 1 (12) 4

Practice #29

저희 동네 도서관에는 희귀한 책이 많습니다.
There are many rare books in my neighborhood library.
[jeo-hui dong-ne do-seo-gwan-e-neun hui-gwi-han chaek-i man-seup-ni-da.]
천 년 전에 만들어진 책도 있습니다.
There is even a book made a thousand years ago.
[cheon nyeon jeon-e man-deul-eo-jin chaek-do it-seup-ni-da.]
이러한 책들은 특별한 곳에 보관합니다.
Books like these are kept in a special place.
[i-reo-han chaek-deul-eun teuk-byeol-han go-se bo-gwan-hap-ni-da.]
직원들만 들어갈 수 있는 곳입니다.
It's a place where only employees can enter.
[jik-won-deul-man deul-eo-gal su it-neun go-ship-ni-da.]
하지만 가끔씩 일반인에게도 공개가 됩니다.
But sometimes it's open to the public.
[ha-ji-man ga-ggeum-ssik il-ban-in-e-ge-do gong-gae-ga doep-ni-da.]
일년에 한 번, 특별한 행사가 있습니다.
Once a year, there's a special event.
[il-nyeon-e han beon, teuk-byeol-han haeng-sa-ga it-seup-ni-da.]
아쉽지만, 사진을 찍을 수 는 없습니다.
Sadly, you can't take a picture.
[a-ship-ji-man, sa-jin-eul jjik-eul su neun eop-seup-ni-da.]
저도 행사에 가 본 적이 있습니다.
I've also been to the event.
[jeo-do haeng-sa-e ga bon jeok-i it-seup-ni-da.]
그 날에는, 다른 나라에서도 손님이 많이 옵니다.
That day, many guests come from different countries.
[geu nal-e-neun, da-reun na-ra-e-seo-do son-nim-i man-i op-ni-da.]
줄이 너무 길어서 한참을 기다렸습니다.
I waited for a long time because the line was too long.
[jul-i neo-mu gil-eo-seo han-cham-eul gi-da-ryeot-seup-ni-da.]
그래도, 그럴만한 가치가 있었습니다.
But still, it was worth doing it.
[geu-rae-do, geu-reol-man-han ga-chi-ga it-seot-seup-ni-da.]
다음 행사는 내년 봄에 있습니다.
The next event is in next spring.

[da-eum haeng-sa-neun nae-nyeon bom-e it-seup-ni-da.]

Answer Keys : (1) 2 (2) 1 (3) 2 (4) 4 (5) 2 (6) 3 (7) 2 (8) 2
(9) 2 (10) 1 (11) 1 (12) 4

Practice #30

자동차는 만 개 이상의 부품으로 만들어집니다.
Cars are made with over ten thousand parts.
[ja-dong-cha-neun man gae i-sang-ui bu-pum-eu-ro man-deul-eo-jip-ni-da.]
대부분 자동으로 조립됩니다.
Most of them are assembled automatically.
[dae-bu-bun ja-dong-eu-ro jo-rip-doep-ni-da.]
자동차를 만드는 것은 시간이 많이 걸리지 않습니다. Making a car doesn't take a lot of time.
[ja-dong-cha-reul man-deu-neun geo-seun shi-gan-i man-i geol-li-ji an-seup-ni-da.]
예전에는 한 달 정도 걸렸습니다.
In the past, it took about a month.
[ye-jeon-e-neun han dal jeong-do geol-ryeot-seup-ni-da.]
모두 사람이 만들어야 했기 때문입니다.
It's because everything had to be made by humans.
[mo-du sa-ram-i man-deul-eo-ya haet-gi ttae-mun-ip-ni-da.]
지금은 약 백분의 일 정도 시간이 걸립니다.
Nowadays it takes about one-hundredth of the time.
[ji-geum-eun yak baek-bun-ui il jeong-do shi-gan-i geol-lip-ni-da.]
기계가 없었으면, 자동차는 매우 비쌌을 겁니다.
If there were no machines, cars would have been very busy.
[gi-gye-ga eop-seot-seu-myeon, ja-dong-cha-neun mae-u bi-ssat-seul geop-ni-da.]
그리고, 자전거를 타는 사람이 더 많았을 겁니다.
And, there would have been more people riding bicycles.
[geu-ri-go, ja-jeon-geo-reul ta-neun sa-ram-i deo man-at-seul geop-ni-da]
물론, 자전거를 타는 것은 건강에 더 좋습니다.
Of course, riding a bicycle is better for health.
[mul-lon, ja-jeon-geo-reul ta-neun geo-seun geon-gang-e deo jot-seup-ni-da.]
하지만, 멀리 가기에는 힘이 듭니다.
But, it's difficult to go far.
[ha-ji-man, meol-li ga-gi-e-neun him-i deup-ni-da.]
자동차는 우리의 생활을 편하게 해줍니다.
Cars make our lives comfortable.
[ja-dong-cha-neun u-ri-ui saeng-hwal-eul pyeon-ha-ge hae-jup-ni-da.]
하지만, 술을 마시고 운전하면 위험합니다.
But, driving after drinking is dangerous.
[ha-ji-man, sul-eul ma-shi-go un-jeon-ha-myeon wi-heom-hap-ni-da.]

Answer Keys : (1) 2 (2) 2 (3) 1 (4) 3 (5) 3 (6) 2 (7) 1 (8) 1
(9) 3 (10) 2 (11) 4 (12) 3

Practice #31 (Difficulty ★★★★☆)

Read the following passage carefully and answer the following questions.

사람은 물론, 동물에게도 습관이 있습니다.
[sa-ram-eun mul-lon, dong-mul-e-ge-do seup-gwan-i it-seup-ni-da.]

그리고 그 습관은 모두 다릅니다.
[geu-ri-go geu seup-gwan-eun mo-du da-reup-ni-da.]

습관은 유전적인 영향도 있고, 후천적인 영향도 있습니다.
[seup-gwan-eun yu-jeon-jeok-in yeong-hyang-do it-go, hu-cheon-jeok-in yeong-hyang-do it-seup-ni-da.]

유전적인 것은, 할아버지 할머니로부터도 영향을 받습니다.
[yu-jeon-jeok-in geo-seun, hal-a-beo-ji hal-meo-ni-ro-bu-teo-do yeong-hyang-eul bat-seup-ni-da.]

후천적인 것은, 태아때부터 만들어 진다고 합니다.
[hu-cheon-jeok-in geo-seun, tae-a-ttae-bu-teo man-deul-eo-jin-da-go hap-ni-da.]

엄마의 행동을 느끼고, 따라합니다.
[eom-ma-ui haeng-dong-eul neu-kki-go, tta-ra-hap-ni-da.]

많은 사람들이 습관은 고칠 수 없다고 믿습니다.
[man-eun sa-ram-deul-i seup-gwan-eun go-chil su eop-da-go mit-seup-ni-da.]

왜냐면 너무 오랜 시간동안 익숙해져있기 때문입니다.
[wae-nya-myeon neo-mu o-raen shi-gan-dong-an ik-suk-hae-jyeo-it-gi ttae-mun-ip-ni-da.]

하지만 습관은 연습을 통해서 고쳐질 수 있습니다.
[ha-ji-man seup-gwan-eun yeon-seup-eul tong-hae-seo go-chyeo-jil su it-seup-ni-da.]

이것은 동물을 대상으로 한 연구로도 밝혀졌습니다.
[i-geo-seun dong-mul-eul dae-sang-eu-ro han yeon-gu-ro-do bal-kyeo-jyeot-seup-ni-da.]

원숭이에게 먹이를 사용한 실험으로, 습관을 고쳤습니다.
[won-sung-i-e-ge meok-i-reul sa-yong-han shil-heom-eu-ro, seup-gwan-eul go-chyeot-seup-ni-da.]

원숭이는 사람과 비슷하기 때문에, 사람도 습관을 고칠 수 있습니다.
[won-sung-i-neun sa-ram-gwa bi-seut-ha-gi ttae-mun-e, sa-ram-do seup-gwan-eul go-chil su it-seup-ni-da.]

Question 1. True or False...? According to the passage, only humans have habits.

1. True 2. False

Question 2. According to the passage, such habits are pretty similar to each other.

1. Car 2. Train 3. Airplane 4. Subway

Question 3. True or False...? According to the passage, habits are affected by hereditary factors only.

1. True 2. False

Question 4. According to the passage, hereditary factors can go as far back as...

1. Parents 2. Grandparents 3. Great-great Parents 4. Current Generation 5. Birth of Human Race

Question 5. According to the passage, the learned/acquired habits are formed as early as...

1. Fetus 2. Infancy 3. First Birthday 4. Third Birthday 5. Tenth Birthday

Question 6. According to the passage, such habits are learned/acquired by mimicking...

1. Mom's Behaviors 2. What's On TV 3. Other Similar Babies 4. What The Grandparents Do 5. Dad's Behaviors

Question 7. True or False...? According to the passage, many people believe habits can't be fixed.

1. True 2. False

Question 8. According to the passage, the reason for the above reasoning is that people...

1. Have Been Used To It For Too Long 2. Don't Want To Make Changes 3. Are Afraid of Changes 4. Lack Motivation 5. Aren't Aware Of Proper Training Methods

Question 9. According to the passage, habits can be fixed with...

1. Learning 2. Studying 3. Punishing 4. Practicing 5. Embarrassing

Question 10. According to the passage, it's been proven by tests involving...

1. Babies 2. Children 3. Animals 4. Plants 5. Insects

Question 11. According to the passage, what was used on the subject during the test?

1. Food 2. Punishment 3. Fear 4. Reward 5. Intimidation

Question 12. According to the passage, the same results can be made because humans are...

1. Unique 2. Similar To Monkeys 3. Smart 4. More Capable 5. More Balanced

Practice #32 (Difficulty ★ ★ ★ ★ ☆)

Read the following passage carefully and answer the following questions.

대한민국에서 가장 큰 도시는 서울입니다.
[dae-han-min-guk-e-seo ga-jang keun do-shi-neun seo-ul-ip-ni-da.]

조선 시대에는 한양이라 불렸습니다.
[jo-seon shi-dae-e-neun han-yang-i-ra bul-lyeot-seup-ni-da.]

서울이라고 불리운 것은 백 년도 되지 않습니다.
[seo-ul-i-ra-go bul-li-un geo-seun baek nyeon-do doe-ji an-seup-ni-da.]

서울은 대한민국의 수도입니다.
[seo-ul-eun dae-han-min-guk-ui su-do-ip-ni-da.]

서울의 인구는 천만 명에 달합니다.
[seo-ul-ui in-gu-neun cheon-man myeong-e dal-hap-ni-da.]

이 것은, 도쿄와 뉴욕보다도 많은 숫자입니다.
[i geo-seun, to-kyo-wa nyu-yok-bo-da-do man-eun sut-ja-ip-ni-da.]

서울에는 다양한 국적의 외국인들이 살고있습니다.
[seo-ul-e-neun da-yang-han guk-jeok-ui oe-guk-in-deul-i sal-go-it-seup-ni-da.]

이태원에 가면, 한국인보다 외국인들이 더 많습니다.
[i-tae-won-e ga-myeon, han-guk-in-bo-da oe-guk-in-deul-i deo man-seup-ni-da.]

서울은 전통과 현대가 함께있는 도시입니다.
[seo-ul-eun jeon-tong-gwa hyeon-dae-ga ham-kke-it-neun do-shi-ip-ni-da.]

하지만 차가 많아 교통이 복잡한 것은 단점입니다.
[ha-ji-man cha-ga man-a gyo-tong-i bok-jap-han geo-seun dan-jeom-ip-ni-da.]

북한과 통일이 되면, 서울이 수도가 될 가능성이 높습니다.
[buk-han-gwa tong-il-i doe-myeon, seo-ul-i su-do-ga doel ga-neung-seong-i nop-seup-ni-da.]

물론, 시민들의 의견이 가장 중요합니다.
[mul-mon, shi-min-deul-ui ui-gyeon-i ga-jang jung-yo-hap-ni-da.]

Question 1. True or False...? The second-largest city in Korea is Seoul.

1. True 2. False

Question 2. According to the passage, what was Seoul called during the Joseon Dynasty?

1. Shi Dae 2. Han Yang 3. Gyeong Seong 4. Seo Ra 5. I Ra

Question 3. True or False...? It's been more than a hundred years since it's been called Seoul.

1. True 2. False

Question 4. According to the passage, which city is the capital of Korea?

1. Seoul 2. Busan 3. Pyong Yang 4. Daegu 5. Sudo

Question 5. According to the passage, the population of Seoul is near...

1. One Million 2. Five Million 3. Ten Million 4. Thirty Million 5. One Billion

Question 6. True or False...? That number is slightly smaller than that of Tokyo or New York.

1. True 2. False

Question 7. According to the passage, there are a lot of people with various THIS living in Seoul.

1. Cultures 2. Blood Types 3. Personalities 4. Nationalities 5. Occupations

Question 8. True or False...? In Itaewon, there are more foreigners than Koreans.

1. True 2. False

Question 9. According to the passage, what exist together in Seoul?

1. Evil and Angel 2. Past and Future 3. Tradition and Modernity 4. North and South Koreans
5. Lights and Shadows

Question 10. According to the passage, what's the downside of Seoul?

1. Heavy Traffic 2. Stores Closing Too Early 3. People Working Too Hard
4. Street Signs Are Difficult To Understand 5. People Are Rude

Question 11. True or False...? If unification took place, the possibility of Seoul becoming the capital is relatively low.

1. True 2. False

Question 12. According to the passage, for the matter above, what's the most important factor?

1. International Politics 2. Domestic Politics 3. Citizens' Opinions 4. Politician's' Votes 5. Tradition

Practice #33 (Difficulty ★ ★ ★ ★ ☆)

Read the following passage carefully and answer the following questions.

병원에 가장 환자가 많은 때는 가을입니다.
[byeong-won-e ga-jang hwan-ja-ga man-eun ttae-neun ga-eul-ip-ni-da.]

계절이 바뀌는 시기라서 그렇습니다.
[gye-jeol-i ba-kkwi-neun shi-gi-ra-seo geu-reot-seup-ni-da.]

아침과 밤의 온도 차이가 심하기 때문에, 감기에 많이 걸립니다.
[a-chim-gwa bam-ui on-do cha-i-ga shim-ha-gi ttae-mun-e, gam-gi-e man-i geol-lip-ni-da.]

감기에 걸리면 수분을 충분히 섭취해야 합니다.
[gam-gi-e geol-li-myeon su-bun-eul chung-bun-hi seop-chwi-hae-ya hap-ni-da.]

따뜻한 차를 마시는 것을 추천합니다.
[tta-tteut-han cha-reul ma-shi-neun geo-seul chu-cheon-hap-ni-da.]

하지만 커피를 마시는 것은 좋지 않습니다.
[ha-ji-man keo-pi-reul ma-shi-neun geo-seun jot-chi an-seup-ni-da.]

커피는 소변을 자주 보게 만들기 때문입니다.
[keo-pi-neun so-byeon-eul ja-ju bo-ge man-deul-gi ttae-mun-ip-ni-da.]

이와 더불어, 과일을 많이 먹는 것도 좋습니다.
[i-wa deo-bul-eo, gwa-il-eul man-i meok-neun geot-do jot-seup-ni-da.]

감기는 전염성이 높은 질병입니다.
[gam-gi-neun jeon-yeon-seong-i nop-eun jil-byeong-ip-ni-da.]

외출하고 집에 돌아오면 손을 잘 씻어야 합니다.
[oe-chul-ha-go jip-e dol-a-o-myeon son-eul jal ssi-seo-ya hap-ni-da.]

기침을 할 때는 입을 가려야 합니다.
[gi-chim-eul hal ttae-neun ip-eul ga-ryeo-ya hap-ni-da.]

감기는 약 일주일 정도 지나면 없어집니다.
[gam-gi-neun yak il-ju-il jeong-do ji-na-myeon eop-seo-jip-ni-da.]

Question 1. According to the passage, hospitals have most patients around...

1. Spring 2. Summer 3. Fall 4. Winter 5. All Year Round

Question 2. According to the passage, what's the reason for it?

1. Contagious Diseases Flourish 2. It's When Medicines Are Cheap 3. It's Holiday Season
4. More Doctors Are Available 5. It's When Seasons Change

Question 3. According to the passage, patients get a cold because...

1. The Day/Night Temperature Difference Is Big 2. People Wear Fewer Clothes 3. People Eat Raw
Foods 4. Viruses Are Stronger 5. Animals With Bacteria Are More Active

Question 4. According to the passage, what should you do when you have a cold?

1. Exercise More 2. Raise Carbs Intake 3. Lower Fat Intake 4. Take Enough Fluids 5. Exercise Less

Question 5. According to the passage, what does the author recommend drinking?

1. Vitamin Water 2. Boiling Water 3. Cold Juice 4. Warm Tea 5. Chicken Soup

Question 6. True or False...? The author claims that drinking coffee is also helpful.

1. True 2. False

Question 7. According to the passage, the reason for the above is because coffee makes you...

1. Stay Alert 2. More Energetic 3. Urinate More 4. Sweat Less 5. Burn More Calories

Question 8. According to the passage, eating lots of THIS is also recommended.

1. Grains 2. Nuts 3. Ice Cream 4. Tofu 5. Fruits

Question 9. According to the passage, what kind of disease is a cold?

1. Scary 2. Deadly 3. Negligible 4. Highly Contagious 5. Mysterious

Question 10. According to the passage, what should you do when you come back home?

1. Brush Teeth 2. Wash Face 3. Sanitize Your Phone 4. Wash Hands 5. Take Off Clothes

Question 11. According to the passage, what do you have to do when you cough?

1. Close Your Eyes 2. Warn Other People 3. Hold Your Breath 4. Cover Your Mouth 5. Sit Down

Question 12. According to the passage, how long would it take for a cold to go away?

1. About Three Days 2. Exactly Four Days 3. Roughly A Week 4. Less Than Ten Days 5. In A Month

Read the following passage carefully and answer the following questions.

화재는 예고 없이 찾아옵니다.
[hwa-jae-neun ye-go eop-shi cha-ja-op-ni-da.]

일상 생활에서 예방 해야합니다.
[il-sang saeng-hwal-e-seo ye-bang hae-ya-hap-ni-da.]

주방에서 불을 사용할때 특히 신경을 써야합니다.
[ju-bang-e-seo bul-eul sa-yong-hal-ttae teuk-hi shin-gyeong-eul sseo-ya-hap-ni-da.]

가스를 끄지 않으면, 작은 불꽃으로도 화재가 발생합니다.
[ga-seu-reul ggeu-ji an-eu-myeon, jak-eun bul-kkot-cheu-ro-do hwa-jae-ga bal-saeng-hap-ni-da.]

화재가 발생하면, 소방서에 신고해야 합니다.
[hwa-jae-ga bal-saeng-ha-myeon, so-bang-seo-e shin-go-hae-ya hap-ni-da.]

그리고, 창문을 모두 열고 사람들에게 알립니다.
[geu-ri-go, chang-mun-eul mo-du yeol-go sa-ram-deul-e-ge al-lip-ni-da.]

소방관이 도착 할 때까지, 침착해야 합니다.
[so-bang-gwan-i do-chak hal ttae-kka-ji, chim-chak-hae-ya hap-ni-da.]

매년 약 오백명의 사람이 화재로 사망합니다.
[mae-nyeon yak o-baek-myeong-ui sa-ram-i hwa-jae-ro sa-mang-hap-ni-da.]

교통사고보다 많은 숫자입니다.
[gyo-tong-sa-go-bo-da man-eun sut-ja-ip-ni-da.]

모든 사고는 예방할 수 있습니다.
[mo-deun sa-go-neun ye-bang-hal su it-seup-ni-da.]

만약을 대비해, 집에 소화기를 사 놓아야 합니다.
[man-yak-eul dae-bi-hae, jip-e so-hwa-gi-reul sa no-a-ya hap-ni-da.]

그리고, 비상구가 어디 있는지 기억해야 합니다.
[geu-ri-go, bi-sang-gu-ga eo-di it-neun-ji gi-eok-hae-ya hap-ni-da.]

Question 1. True or False...? According to the passage, there are obvious signs before a fire breaks out.

1. True 2. False

Question 2. True or False...? There is nothing that can be done to prevent a fire.

1. True 2. False

Question 3. According to the passage, you have to be especially careful when using fire in the...

1. Military 2. Bathroom 3. Kitchen 4. Bedroom 5. Gas Station

Question 4. According to the passage, doing THIS can start a fire with just a little spark.

1. Not Opening Windows 2. Not Closing The Door 3. Not Opening The Freezer
4. Not Operating The Exhaust Fan 5. Not Shutting Off The Gas

Question 5. According to the passage, what should you do if a fire breaks out?

1. Call The Police 2. Call Parents 3. Notify The Neighbors 4. Call The Fire Department
5. Put Out The Fire Using Fire Extinguisher

Question 6. According to the passage, what else should you do after opening the window?

1. Take Valuables To Safe Place 2. Climb Down The Ladder 3. Notify People 4. Let The Fire Crew In

Question 7. True or False...? Until the firemen arrive, you have to do stay alert.

1. True 2. False

Question 8. According to the passage, how many people die every year in a fire?

1. About 100 2. About 300 3. About 500 4. About 1,000 5. About 5,000

Question 9. According to the passage, the number above is greater than the number from...

1. Car Accidents 2. Airplane Crashes 3. Drowning 4. Electric Shock 5. Homicide

Question 10. According to the passage, all accidents can be prevented.

1. True 2. False

Question 11. According to the passage, what should you buy and keep at home?

1. Insurance Policy 2. Medical Kit 3. Emergency Flash Light 4. Fire Extinguisher 5. Water Hose

Question 12. According to the passage, you also have to remember where THIS is...

1. Emergency Exit 2. Valuables 3. Fire Extinguisher 4. Telephone 5. Emergency Ladder

Practice #35 (Difficulty ★★★★☆)

Read the following passage carefully and answer the following questions.

여행을 할 때는 소지품을 분실하는 경우가 많습니다.
[yeo-haeng-eul hal ttae-neun so-ji-pum-eul bun-shil-ha-neun gyeong-u-ga man-seup-ni-da.]

설문조사에 따르면, 지갑을 가장 많이 잃어버린다고 합니다.
[seol-mun-jo-sa-e tta-reu-myeon, ji-gap-eul ga-jang man-i il-eo-beo-rin-da-go hap-ni-da.]

주로 관광지에서 소매치기를 당한다고 합니다.
[ju-ro gwan-gwang-ji-e-seo so-mae-chi-gi-reul dang-han-da-go hap-ni-da.]

외국에서는 언어가 통하지 않아서 문제 해결이 쉽지 않습니다.
[oe-guk-e-seo-neun eon-eo-ga tong-ha-ji an-a-seo mun-je hae-gyeol-i ship-ji an-seup-ni-da.]

경찰서에 가도 큰 도움이 되지 않습니다.
[gyeong-chal-seo-e ga-do keun do-um-i doe-ji an-seup-ni-da.]

그래서 지갑은 옷의 안쪽 주머니에 넣는것이 좋습니다.
[geu-rae-seo ji-gap-eun o-sui an-jjok ju-meo-ni-e neot-neun geo-shi jot-seup-ni-da.]

돈을 한번에 모두 가지고 다니는 것도 좋지 않습니다.
[don-eul han-beon-e mo-du ga-ji-go da-ni-neun geot-do jot-chi an-seup-ni-da.]

큰 돈은 호텔 금고에 보관해야 합니다.
[keun don-eun ho-tel geum-go-e bo-gwan-hae-ya hap-ni-da.]

여권을 잃어버리면, 영사관에 가야합니다.
[yeo-gwon-eul il-eo-beo-ri-myeon, yeong-sa-gwan-e ga-ya-hap-ni-da.]

여권을 다시 만들려면 보통 일주일 정도 시간이 걸립니다.
[yeo-gwon-eul da-shi man-deul-lyeo-myeon bo-tong il-ju-il jeong-do shi-gan-i geol-lip-ni-da.]

하지만 특수한 경우에는 당일에도 만들 수 있습니다.
[ha-ji-man teuk-su-han gyeong-u-e-neun dang-il-e-do man-deul su it-seup-ni-da.]

여행자 보험을 듣는 것은 필수입니다.
[yeo-haeng-ja bo-heom-eul deut-neun geo-seun pil-su-ip-ni-da.]

Question 1. According to the passage, people often lose their belonging when...

1. Shopping 2. Studying 3. Watching a Movie 4. Working Out At The Gym 5. Traveling

Question 2. According to the passage, the survey results revealed that people lose THIS the most...

1. Passport 2. Wallet 3. I.D. Card 4. Phone 5. Credit Card

Question 3. True or False...? Most of the incidents take place as a result of...

1. Pick Pocket 2. Robbery 3. Negligence 4. Language Barrier 5. Breaking The Local Law

Question 4. According to the passage, why is it difficult to resolve a problem when abroad?

1. Time Difference 2. Cultural Difference 3. Laws Are Different 4. Language Barrier 5. Xenophobia

Question 5. True or False...? For such problems, the police station is the best place to get help.

1. True 2. False

Question 6. According to the passage, it's best to put your wallet in...

1. Inside Pocket of Your Clothes 2. The Safe Box 3. Your Back Pack 4. The Car 5. Your Shoes

Question 7. True or False...? It's better to carry around all of your money at the same time.

1. True 2. False

Question 8. According to the passage, where should you keep a large amount of money?

1. Friend's Place 2. Hotel Safety Box 3. Bank Account 4. Underneath a Bed 5. Car Trunk

Question 9. According to the passage, where should you go if you lose your passport?

1. Lost and Found 2. Police Station 3. Governor's Office 4. City Hall 5. Embassy

Question 10. According to the passage, how long does it usually take to make a new passport?

1. A Few Days 2. About Five Days 3. About a Week 4. About Two Weeks 5. About a Month

Question 11. True or False...? There is no way to have the passport-making process expedited.

1. True 2. False

Question 12. True or False...? The author claims that getting traveler's insurance is a must.

1. True 2. False

Practice #36 (Difficulty ★ ★ ★ ★ ☆)

Read the following passage carefully and answer the following questions.

노래를 부르는 것은 건강에 이롭습니다.
[no-rae-reul bu-reu-neun geo-seun geon-gang-e i-rop-seun-ni-da.]

심리적으로도 그렇고, 육체적으로도 그렇습니다.
[shim-li-jeok-eu-ro-do geu-reot-go, yuk-che-jeok-eu-ro-do geu-reot-seup-ni-da.]

노래를 부르면, 혈액순환이 활발해집니다.
[no-rae-reul bu-reu-myeon, hyeol-aek-sun-hwan-i hwal-bal-hae-jip-ni-da.]

행복을 느끼는 호르몬도 나옵니다.
[haeng-bok-eul neu-kki-neun ho-reu-mon-do na-op-ni-da.]

큰 소리로 노래를 부르면, 효과가 더욱 좋습니다.
[keun so-ri-ro no-rae-reul bu-reu-myeon, hyo-gwa-ga deo-uk jot-seup-ni-da.]

연구에 따르면, 동물들도 노래를 부를 수 있다고 합니다.
[yeon-gu-e tta-reu-myeon, dong-mul-deul-do no-rae-reul bu-reul su it-da-go hap-ni-da.]

기분이 좋을때와 나쁠때, 목소리가 다릅니다.
[gi-bun-i jo-eul-ttae-wa na-bbeul-ttae, mok-so-ri-ga da-reup-ni-da.]

그리고, 뇌의 반응도 다릅니다.
[geu-ri-go, noe-ui ban-eung-do da-reup-ni-da.]

이 것은, 과학이 발전했기 때문에 가능한 것입니다.
[i geo-seun, gwa-hak-i bal-jeon-haet-gi ttae-mun-e ga-neung-han geo-ship-ni-da.]

예전에는, 동물에게는 감정이 없다고 생각했습니다.
[ye-jeon-e-neun, dong-mul-e-ge-neun gam-jeong-i eop-da-go saeng-gak-haet-seup-ni-da.]

이제는, 동물의 언어를 분석하기 위해 연구 중입니다.
[i-je-neun, dong-mul-ui eon-eo-reul bun-seok-ha-gi wi-hae yeon-gu-jung-ip-ni-da.]

십년 안에, 동물과 인간은 대화를 나눌 수 있을 것입니다.
[ship-nyeon an-e, dong-mul-gwa in-gan-eun dae-hwa-reul na-nul su it-seul geo-ship-ni-da.]

Question 1. According to the passage, doing THIS is beneficial for your health.

1. Jumping Ropes 2. Walking 3. Praying 4. Singing 5. Taking The Stairs Instead of Elevator

Question 2. True or False...? Doing such activity is beneficial both physically and mentally.

1. True 2. False

Question 3. According to the passage, doing such activity facilitates THIS.

1. Immune System 2. Blood Circulation 3. Brain Activity 4. Hormone Release 5. Aging

Question 4. According to the passage, doing such activity makes the body release hormone that's associated with...

1. Fear 2. Excitement 3. Vision 4. Happiness 5. Sadness

Question 5. According to the passage, it's even more effective if you...

1. Sing Loud 2. Walk Fast 3. Take a Break 4. Do It On a Regular Basis 5. Do It With Friends

Question 6. True or False...? According to a study, animals are not capable of singing.

1. True 2. False

Question 7. True or False...? According to a study, animals have different voices when happy and not happy.

1. True 2. False

Question 8. True or False...? According to the passage, their brains, however, don't show any difference.

1. True 2. False

Question 9. True or False...? Such discovery was made without the help of technology.

1. True 2. False

Question 10. True or False...? Animals have long been believed to have emotions, just like humans.

1. True 2. False

Question 11. According to the passage, what is being researched for analysis?

1. Animal Language 2. Animal Instincts 3. Human Telepathy 4. Supernatural Beings 5. Plant Growth

Question 12. According to the passage, humans and animals can talk to each other within...

1. Three Years 2. Ten Years 3. Twenty Years 4. Fifty Years 5. Never

Practice #37 (Difficulty ★ ★ ★ ★ ☆)

Read the following passage carefully and answer the following questions.

인구 중 절반 이상이 아침 식사를 하지 못한다고 합니다.
[in-gu jung jeol-ban i-sang-i a-chim shik-sa-reul ha-ji mot-han-da-go hap-ni-da.]

아침 식사는 하루 중 가장 중요한 식사입니다.
[a-chim shik-sa-neun ha-ru jung ga-jang jung-yo-han shik-sa-ip-ni-da.]

우리의 뇌가 깨어나는 시간이기 때문입니다.
[u-ri-ui noe-ga kkae-eo-na-neun shi-gan-i-gi ttae-mun-ip-ni-da.]

실제로, 아침 식사를 하는 학생들의 성적이 더욱 좋습니다.
[shil-je-ro, a-chim shik-sa-reul ha-neun hak-saeng-deul-ui seong-jeok-i deo-uk jot-seup-ni-da.]

그 중에서도 수학 성적이 차이가 많이 납니다.
[geu jung-e-seo-do su-hak seong-jeok-i cha-i-ga man-i nap-ni-da.]

조금이라도 아침 식사를 하는 것이, 하지 않는 것 보다 좋습니다.
[jo-geum-i-ra-do a-chim shik-sa-reul ha-neun geo-shi, ha-ji an-neun geot bo-da jot-seup-ni-da.]

우유 한 잔을 마셔도 큰 도움이 됩니다.
[u-yu han jan-eul ma-shyeo-do keun do-um-i doep-ni-da.]

하지만 아침을 너무 많이 먹으면, 잠이 오게 될 수 있습니다.
[ha-ji-man, a-chim-eul neo-mu man-i meok-eu-myeon, jam-i o-ge doel su it-seup-ni-da.]

아침 식사를 하지 못하면, 점심을 많이 먹게 될 수 있습니다.
[a-chim shik-sa-reul ha-ji mot-ha-myeon, jeom-shim-eul man-i meok-ge doel su it-seup-ni-da.]

이것은 비만의 원인이 될 수 있습니다.
[i-geo-seun bi-man-ui won-in-i doel su it-seup-ni-da.]

하루 전 날 저녁, 다음날 아침 식사를 미리 만드는 것도 좋습니다.
[ha-ru jeon nal jeo-nyeok, da-eum-nal a-chim shik-sa-reul mi-ri man-deu-neun geot-do jot-seup-ni-da.]

아침에 바쁜 사람들에게 특히 그렇습니다.
[a-chim-e ba-bbeun sa-ram-deul-e-ge teuk-hi geu-reot-seup-ni-da.]

Question 1. According to the passage, how much of the population can't have breakfast?

1. 25% 2. 30% 3. 50% 4. 75% 5. 85%

Question 2. According to the passage, the most important meal of the day is...?

1. Breakfast 2. Brunch 3. Lunch 4. Dinner 5. Late Dinner

Question 3. True or False...? It is so because it's when THIS wakes up.

1. Sensory Organs 2. Body 3. Brain 4. Emotions 5. Instincts

Question 4. True or False...? Students who skip breakfast get better grades.

1. True 2. False

Question 5. According to the passage, on which subject is the difference biggest?

1. Korean 2. English 3. Math 4. Chemistry 5. P.E.

Question 6. True or False...? It's better to entirely skip breakfast than have just a small amount of breakfast.

1. True 2. False

Question 7. True or False...? Drinking a glass of milk is a big help.

1. True 2. False

Question 8. According to the passage, having too much for breakfast can make you...

1. Alert 2. Tired 3. Jittery 4. Excited 5. Sleepy

Question 9. According to the passage, what might happen if you can't have breakfast?

1. Eat Too Much For Lunch 2. Fall Asleep 3. Become Angry 4. Become Sensitive 5. Lose Motivation

Question 10. What can be caused as a result of the above?

1. Anger 2. Fatigue 3. Obesity 4. Anorexia 5. Toxic Build-Up

Question 11. According to the passage, what is suggested to be done the night before?

1. Eat In Advance 2. Do The Groceries 3. Make Breakfast In Advance
4. Write Down What You Ate Throughout The Day 5. Go To Bed Early

Question 12. According to the passage, the method above is especially helpful for those who are...

1. Lazy 2. Easily Tired 3. Busy In The Morning 4. Economically Challenged 5. Less Motivated

Read the following passage carefully and answer the following questions.

한국의 예절은 생각보다 복잡합니다.
[han-guk-ui ye-jeol-eun saeng-gak-bo-da bok-jap-hap-ni-da.]

특히 어른들과 술을 마실 때에는 신경을 써야합니다.
[teuk-hi eo-reun-deul-gwa sul-eul ma-shil ttae-e-neun shin-gyeong-eul sseo-ya-hap-ni-da.]

의도와는 다르게, 예의 없는 사람으로 보일 수 있습니다.
[ui-do-wa-neun da-reu-ge, ye-ui eop-neun sa-ram-eu-ro bo-il su it-seup-ni-da.]

어른께 술을 따라드릴 때에는, 두 손으로 해야 합니다.
[eo-reun-kke sul-eul tta-ra-deu-ril ttae-e-neun, du son-eu-ro hae-ya hap-ni-da.]

어른으로부터 술을 받을때도, 두 손을 사용해야 합니다.
[eo-reun-eu-ro-bu-teo sul-eul bat-eul ttae-do, du son-eul sa-yong-hae-ya hap-ni-da.]

하지만 외국인이 실수하면, 너그럽게 용서합니다.
[ha-ji-man oe-guk-in-i shil-su-ha-myeon, neo-geu-reop-ge yong-seo-hap-ni-da.]

한국어의 존댓말 또한 굉장히 복잡합니다.
[han-guk-eo-ui jon-daet-mal tto-han goeng-jang-hi bok-jap-hap-ni-da.]

어른들과 친구에게 사용하는 단어가 다릅니다.
[eo-reun-deul-gwa chin-gu-e-ge sa-yong-ha-neun dan-eo-ga da-reup-ni-da.]

한국인들도 가끔씩 틀릴 때가 있습니다.
[han-guk-in-deul-do ga-kkeum-ssik teul-lil ttae-ga it-seup-ni-da.]

특히 드라마나 영화에서도 틀리게 쓰이는 것을 볼 수 있습니다.
[teuk-hi deu-ra-ma-na yeong-hwa-e-seo-do teul-li-ge sseu-i-neun geo-seul bol su it-seup-ni-da.]

하지만 진짜 예의는 마음에서 나옵니다.
[ha-ji-man jin-jja ye-ui-neun ma-eum-e-seo na-op-ni-da.]

어려서부터 타인을 존중하는 교육을 해야합니다.
[eo-ryeo-seo-bu-teo ta-in-eul jon-jung-ha-neun gyo-yuk-eul hae-ya-hap-ni-da.]

Question 1. True or False...? Korean manners are less complicated than you think.

1. True 2. False

Question 2. According to the passage, you have to pay special attention to your manners when you are...

1. Drinking With Older People 2. Eating With Relatives 3. Playing With Children 4. Talking To Teachers 5. Ordering Something Over The Phone

Question 3. If you don't do as mentioned above, you might be seen as someone who is...

1. Rude 2. Ignorant 3. Arrogant 4. Insensitive 5. Angry

Question 4. True or False...? When pouring liquor to older people, you have to use both hands.

1. True 2. False

Question 5. True or False...? When receiving liquor from older people, you can use one hand.

1. True 2. False

Question 6. True or False...? People are more strict on foreigners when it comes to manners.

1. True 2. False

Question 7. According to the passage, what else is very complicated?

1. Korean Culture 2. Korean Honorifics 3. Korean Pronunciation 4. Korean History 5. Korean Names

Question 8. True or False...? There are different words used to older people and to friends.

1. True 2. False

Question 9. True or False...? Thanks to early education, Korean people don't make such mistakes.

1. True 2. False

Question 10. According to the passage, such mistakes can also be seen on/in...

1. Drama and Movies 2. Music Lyrics 3. Textbooks 4. Radio 5. Traditional Wedding

Question 11. According to the passage, where do real manners come from?

1. Brain 2. Habit 3. Heart 4. Experience 5. Behaviors

Question 12. True or False...? According to the author, it's important to educate how to respect others at an early age.

1. True 2. False

Read the following passage carefully and answer the following questions.

축구는 세계에서 가장 인기있는 종목입니다.
[chuk-gu-neun se-gye-e-seo ga-jang in-gi-it-neun jong-mok-ip-ni-da.]

남녀노소 관계 없이, 누구나 좋아합니다.
[nam-nyeo-no-so gwan-gye eop-shi, nu-gu-na jo-a-hap-ni-da.]

규칙이 간단한 것이 가장 큰 인기 이유입니다.
[gyu-chik-i gan-dan-han geo-shi ga-jang keun in-gi i-yu-ip-ni-da.]

공만 있으면 즐길 수 있습니다.
[gong-man it-seu-myeon jeul-gil su it-seup-ni-da.]

간단한 규칙과는 다르게, 다양한 기술이 필요합니다.
[gan-dan-han gy-chik-gwa-neun da-reu-ge, da-yang-han gi-sul-i pil-yo-hap-ni-da.]

빠르게 달리기는 무엇보다 중요합니다.
[bba-reu-ge dal-li-gi-neun mu-eot-bo-da jung-yo-hap-ni-da.]

정확하게 공을 발로 차는 능력도 필요합니다.
[jeong-hwak-ha-ge gong-eul bal-lo cha-neun neung-ryeok-do pil-yo-hap-ni-da.]

쉬지 않고 달릴 수 있는 지구력도 필요합니다.
[shwi-ji an-ko dal-lil su it-neun ji-gu-ryeok-do pil-yo-hap-ni-da.]

모두 연습을 통해 발달 시킬 수 있습니다.
[mo-du yeon-seup-eul tong-hae bal-dal shi-kil su it-seup-ni-da.]

하지만 누구나 똑같은 재능을 갖고 있지 않습니다.
[ha-ji-man nu-gu-na ttok-gat-eun jae-neung-eul gat-go it-ji an-seup-ni-da.]

그래서 각각 다른 역할을 맡아야 합니다.
[geu-rae-seo gak-gak da-reun yeok-hal-eul mat-a-ya hap-ni-da.]

수비와 공격으로 나누어 연습합니다.
[su-bi-wa gong-gyeok-eu-ro na-nu-eo yeon-seup-hap-ni-da.]

Question 1. According to the passage, what is the most popular sport in the world?

1. Baseball 2. Basketball 3. Archery 4. Tae Kwon Do 5. Soccer

Question 2. True or False...? It's mostly liked by the younger population.

1. True 2. False

Question 3. According to the passage, the biggest reason for its popularity is the simplicity of...

1. Uniforms 2. Equipment 3. Rules 4. Philosophy 5. History

Question 4. True or False...? It can be enjoyed as long as you have a ball and sticks.

1. True 2. False

Question 5. True or False...? Just like the simplicity of the sport, it doesn't require many skills.

1. True 2. False

Question 6. According to the passage, what's important than anything else?

1. Running Fast 2. Jumping High 3. Predicting Others' Moves 4. Body Balance 5. Kicking Hard

Question 7. True or False...? Kicking the ball precisely is not really necessary since the ball is quite large.

1. True 2. False

Question 8. According to the passage, THIS is also needed to run continuously.

1. Strong Will 2. Technique 3. Body Coordination 4. Endurance 5. High-Quality Shoes

Question 9. True or False...? According to the passage, only kicking the ball precisely can be improved with practice.

1. True 2. False

Question 10. True or False...? According to the passage, everybody has a similar set of talents in the beginning.

1. True 2. False

Question 11. According to the passage, what is assigned as a result of the above?

1. Numbers 2. Colors 3. Uniforms 4. Roles 5. Teams

Question 12. According to the passage, they are divided into THESE when practicing.

1. Defense and Offense 2. Players and Management 3. Players and Coach 4. Defense and Semi Defense

Practice #40 (Difficulty ★ ★ ★ ★ ☆)

Read the following passage carefully and answer the following questions.

태권도는 매우 세계적인 무예입니다.
[tae-kwon-do-neun mae-u se-gye-jeok-in mu-ye-ip-ni-da.]

팔천만명이 넘는 사람들이 배우고 있습니다.
[pal-cheon-man-myeong-i neom-neun sa-ram-deul-i bae-u-go it-seup-ni-da.]

손과 발을 주로 쓰지만, 발을 더욱 많이 사용합니다.
[son-gwa bal-eul ju-ro sseu-ji-man, bal-eul deo-uk man-i sa-yong-hap-ni-da]

태권도는 타인을 공격하는 것이 목적이 아닙니다.
[tae-kwon-do-neun ta-in-eul gong-gyeok-han-neun geo-shi mok-jeok-i a-nip-ni-da.]

자신의 마음을 단련하는 것이 목표입니다.
[ja-shin-ui ma-eum-eul dan-ryeon-ha-neun geo-shi mok-pyo-ip-ni-da.]

그렇게 하면, 몸과 마음 모두 건강해 질 수 있습니다.
[geu-reot-ge ha-myeon, mom-gwa ma-eum mo-du geon-gang-hae jil su it-seup-ni-da.]

태권도는 올림픽 정식 종목입니다.
[tae-kwon-do-neun ol-lim-pik jeong-shik jong-mok-ip-ni-da.]

요즘에는 외국 선수들도 일등을 많이 합니다.
[yo-jeum-e-neun oe-guk seon-su-deul-do il-deung-eul man-i hap-ni-da.]

한국의 태권도 선생님이 외국에서 학생들을 많이 가르치기 때문입니다.
[han-guk-ui tae-kwon-do seon-saeng-nim-i oe-guk-e-seo hak-saeng-deul-eul man-i ga-reu-chi-gi ttae-mun-ip-ni-da.]

태권도를 배우고, 한국에 대한 관심이 생긴 외국인들이 많습니다.
[tae-kwon-do-reul bae-u-go, han-guk-e dae-han gwan-shim-i saeng-gin oe-guk-in-deul-i man-seup-ni-da.]

그들은 직접 한국을 방문해 태권도의 역사를 공부합니다.
[geu-deul-eun jik-jeop han-guk-eul bang-mun-hae tae-kwon-do-ui yeok-sa-reul gong-bu-hap-ni-da.]

태권도는 한국의 자랑스러운 수출품 입니다.
[tae-kwon-do-neun han-guk-ui ja-rang-seu-reo-un su-chul-pum ip-ni-da.]

Question 1. True or False...? Tae Kwon Do is not well known around the globe.

1. True 2. False

Question 2. According to the passage, over how many people are learning Tae Kwon Do?

1. Five Million 2. Ten Million 3. Fifty Million 4. Eighty Million 5. One Billion

Question 3. True or False...? Tae Kwon Do uses the fist more than the foot.

1. True 2. False

Question 4. True or False...? The purpose of Tae Kwon Do is to be able to attack others before they attack you.

1. True 2. False

Question 5. According to the passage, the goal of Tae Kwon Do is to...

1. Train One's Mind 2. Lose Fat 3. Learn Korean Culture 4. Learn To Respect Others 5. Have No Fear

Question 6. As a result of achieving the goal above, you can make your...

1. Body Healthy 2. Mind Healthy 3. Both Body and Mind Healthy 4. Core Stronger 5. Muscles Harder

Question 7. True or False...? Tae Kwon Do will soon become an official Olympic event.

1. True 2. False

Question 8. True or False...? Foreign players are winning first place a lot nowadays.

1. True 2. False

Question 9. According to the passage, the reason for the above is because...

1. Students Can Learn Using The Internet 2. Korean Instructors Teach Students Overseas 3. Foreign Students Come To Korea To Learn 4. Rules Have Been Modified In Favor of Foreign Players

Question 10. After learning Tae Kwon Do, a lot of foreign students became...

1. Interested In Korea 2. Less Curious About Korean Culture 3. Addicted To Korean Culture
4. Tae Kwon Do Instructors 5. More Spiritually Awake

Question 11. According to the passage, they visit Korea to study...

1. Korean History 2. History of Tae Kwon Do 3. Korean Culture 4. Tae Kwon Do Forms 5. Meditation

Question 12. According to the passage, Tae Kwon Do is Korea's proud...

1. Culture 2. Export 3. Service 4. Sport 5. Asset

Practice #31

사람은 물론, 동물에게도 습관이 있습니다.
Not just humans, but animals have habits also.
[sa-ram-eun mul-lon, dong-mul-e-ge-do seup-gwan-i it-seup-ni-da.]
그리고 그 습관은 모두 다릅니다.
And they are all different.
[geu-ri-go geu seup-gwan-eun mo-du da-reup-ni-da.]
습관은 유전적인 영향도 있고, 후천적인 영향도 있습니다.
Habits have hereditary effects, and also have acquired effects.
[seup-gwan-eun yu-jeon-jeok-in yeong-hyang-do it-go, hu-cheon-jeok-in yeong-hyang-do it-seup-ni-da.]
유전적인 것은, 할아버지 할머니로부터도 영향을 받습니다.
Hereditary ones are influenced by grandfather and grandmother as well.
[yu-jeon-jeok-in geo-seun, hal-a-beo-ji hal-meo-ni-ro-bu-teo-do yeong-hyang-eul bat-seup-ni-da.]
후천적인 것은, 태아때부터 만들어 진다고 합니다.
Acquired ones are made from infancy.
[hu-cheon-jeok-in geo-seun, tae-a-ttae-bu-teo man-deul-eo-jin-da-go hap-ni-da.]
엄마의 행동을 느끼고, 따라합니다.
(Babies) feel their mother's behaviors, and mimic them.
[eom-ma-ui haeng-dong-eul neu-kki-go, tta-ra-hap-ni-da.]
많은 사람들이 습관은 고칠 수 없다고 믿습니다.
Lots of people believe that habits can't be fixed.
[man-eun sa-ram-deul-i seup-gwan-eun go-chil su eop-da-go mit-seup-ni-da.]
왜냐면 너무 오랜 시간동안 익숙해져있기 때문입니다.
It's because we are used to them for too long.
[wae-nya-myeon neo-mu o-raen shi-gan-dong-an ik-suk-hae-jyeo-it-gi ttae-mun-ip-ni-da.]
하지만 습관은 연습을 통해서 고쳐질 수 있습니다.
But habits can be fixed through practice.
[ha-ji-man seup-gwan-eun yeon-seup-eul tong-hae-seo go-chyeo-jil su it-seup-ni-da.]
이것은 동물을 대상으로 한 연구로도 밝혀졌습니다.
This has been confirmed by tests done on animals.
[i-geo-seun dong-mul-eul dae-sang-eu-ro han yeon-gu-ro-do bal-kyeo-jyeot-seup-ni-da.]
원숭이에게 먹이를 사용한 실험으로, 습관을 고쳤습니다.
Tests on monkeys using food fixed their habits.
[won-sung-i-e-ge meok-i-reul sa-yong-han shil-heom-eu-ro, seup-gwan-eul go-chyeot-seup-ni-da.]
원숭이는 사람과 비슷하기 때문에, 사람도 습관을 고칠 수 있습니다.
Because monkeys are similar to humans, humans' habits can be fixed.
[won-sung-i-neun sa-ram-gwa bi-seut-ha-gi ttae-mun-e, sa-ram-do seup-gwan-eul go-chil su it-seup-ni-da.]

Answer Keys : (1) 2 (2) 2 (3) 2 (4) 2 (5) 1 (6) 1 (7) 1 (8) 1 (9) 4 (10) 3 (11) 1 (12) 2

Practice #32

대한민국에서 가장 큰 도시는 서울입니다.
The largest city in Korea is Seoul.
[dae-han-min-guk-e-seo ga-jang keun do-shi-neun seo-ul-ip-ni-da.]
조선 시대에는 한양이라 불렸습니다.
It was called Hanyang during the Joseon era.
[jo-seon shi-dae-e-neun han-yang-i-ra bul-lyeot-seup-ni-da.]
서울이라고 불리운 것은 백 년도 되지 않습니다.
It's been just less than one hundred years since it's been called Seoul.
[seo-ul-i-ra-go bul-li-un geo-seun baek nyeon-do doe-ji an-seup-ni-da.]
서울은 대한민국의 수도입니다.
Seoul is the capital of Korea.
[seo-ul-eun dae-han-min-guk-ui su-do-ip-ni-da.]
서울의 인구는 천만 명에 달합니다.
The population of Seoul is close to ten thousand people.
[seo-ul-ui in-gu-neun cheon-man myeong-e dal-hap-ni-da.]
이 것은, 도쿄와 뉴욕보다도 많은 숫자입니다.
This is, a number even larger than Tokyo and New York.
[i geo-seun, to-kyo-wa nyu-yok-bo-da-do man-eun sut-ja-ip-ni-da.]
서울에는 다양한 국적의 외국인들이 살고있습니다.
There are foreigners with various nationalities living in Seoul
[seo-ul-e-neun da-yang-han guk-jeok-ui oe-guk-in-deul-i sal-go-it-seup-ni-da.]
이태원에 가면, 한국인보다 외국인들이 더 많습니다.
If you go to Itaewon, there are more foreigners than Koreans.
[i-tae-won-e ga-myeon, han-guk-in-bo-da oe-guk-in-deul-i deo man-seup-ni-da.]
서울은 전통과 현대가 함께있는 도시입니다.
Seoul is a city where tradition and modernity exist together.
[seo-ul-eun jeon-tong-gwa hyeon-dae-ga ham-kke-it-neun do-shi-ip-ni-da.]
하지만 차가 많아 교통이 복잡한 것은 단점입니다.
But the downside is the traffic jam caused by a large number of cars.
[ha-ji-man cha-ga man-a gyo-tong-i bok-jap-han geo-seun dan-jeom-ip-ni-da.]
북한과 통일이 되면, 서울이 수도가 될 가능성이 높습니다.
If unified with North Korea, it's highly probable that Seoul will be the capital.
[buk-han-gwa tong-il-i doe-myeon, seo-ul-i su-do-ga doel ga-neung-seong-i nop-seup-ni-da.]
물론, 시민들의 의견이 가장 중요합니다.
Of course, citizens' opinions are the most important.
[mul-mon, shi-min-deul-ui ui-gyeon-i ga-jang jung-yo-hap-ni-da.]

Answer Keys : (1) 2 (2) 2 (3) 2 (4) 1 (5) 3 (6) 2 (7) 4 (8) 1 (9) 3 (10) 1 (11) 2 (12) 3

Practice #33

병원에 가장 환자가 많은 때는 가을입니다.
The time when there are most patients are in the hospital is Fall.
[byeong-won-e ga-jang hwan-ja-ga man-eun ttae-neun ga-eul-ip-ni-da.]
계절이 바뀌는 시기라서 그렇습니다.
It's because it's the time when seasons change.
[gye-jeol-i ba-kkwi-neun shi-gi-ra-seo geu-reot-seup-ni-da.]
아침과 밤의 온도 차이가 심하기 때문에, 감기에 많이 걸립니다.
Because the temperature difference between morning and night is drastic, many catch a cold.
[a-chim-gwa bam-ui on-do cha-i-ga shim-ha-gi ttae-mun-e, gam-gi-e man-i geol-lip-ni-da.]
감기에 걸리면 수분을 충분히 섭취해야 합니다.
If you catch a cold, you need to drink lots of fluid.
[gam-gi-e geol-li-myeon su-bun-eul chung-bun-hi seop-chwi-hae-ya hap-ni-da.]
따뜻한 차를 마시는 것을 추천합니다.
(I) recommend drinking warm tea.
[tta-tteut-han cha-reul ma-shi-neun geo-seul chu-cheon-hap-ni-da.]
하지만 커피를 마시는 것은 좋지 않습니다.
But drinking coffee is not good.
[ha-ji-man keo-pi-reul ma-shi-neun geo-seun jot-chi an-seup-ni-da.]
커피는 소변을 자주 보게 만들기 때문입니다.
It's because coffee makes you urinate often.
[keo-pi-neun so-byeon-eul ja-ju bo-ge man-deul-gi ttae-mun-ip-ni-da.]
이와 더불어, 과일을 많이 먹는 것도 좋습니다.
On top of it, eating fruits is also good.
[i-wa deo-bul-eo, gwa-il-eul man-i meok-neun geot-do jot-seup-ni-da.]
감기는 전염성이 높은 질병입니다.
Cold is a contagious disease.
[gam-gi-neun jeon-yeon-seong-i nop-eun jil-byeong-ip-ni-da.]
외출하고 집에 돌아오면 손을 잘 씻어야 합니다.
If you come from outside, you need to wash your hands carefully.
[oe-chul-ha-go jip-e dol-a-o-myeon son-eul jal ssi-seo-ya hap-ni-da.]
기침을 할 때는 입을 가려야 합니다.
When coughing, you need to cover your mouth.
[gi-chim-eul hal ttae-neun ip-eul ga-ryeo-ya hap-ni-da.]
감기는 약 일주일 정도 지나면 없어집니다.
The cold usually disappears after about a week.
[gam-gi-neun yak il-ju-il jeong-do ji-na-myeon eop-seo-jip-ni-da.]

Answer Keys : (1) 3 (2) 5 (3) 1 (4) 4 (5) 4 (6) 2 (7) 3 (8) 5
(9) 4 (10) 4 (11) 4 (12) 3

Practice #34

화재는 예고 없이 찾아옵니다.
A fire breaks out without warning.
[hwa-jae-neun ye-go eop-shi cha-ja-op-ni-da.]
일상 생활에서 예방 해야합니다.
You need to prevent it in daily life.
[il-sang saeng-hwal-e-seo ye-bang hae-ya-hap-ni-da.]
주방에서 불을 사용할때 특히 신경을 써야합니다.
You have to pay special attention when using a fire in the kitchen.
[ju-bang-e-seo bul-eul sa-yong-hal-ttae teuk-hi shin-gyeong-eul sseo-ya-hap-ni-da.]
가스를 끄지 않으면, 작은 불꽃으로도 화재가 발생합니다.
If you don't turn off gas, a fire can break out even because of a small spark.
[ga-seu-reul ggeu-ji an-eu-myeon, jak-eun bul-kkot-cheu-ro-do hwa-jae-ga bal-saeng-hap-ni-da.]
화재가 발생하면, 소방서에 신고해야 합니다.
If a fire breaks out, you need to report it to the fire department.
[hwa-jae-ga bal-saeng-ha-myeon, so-bang-seo-e shin-go-hae-ya hap-ni-da.]
그리고, 창문을 모두 열고 사람들에게 알립니다.
And, open all windows and notify people.
[geu-ri-go, chang-mun-eul mo-du yeol-go sa-ram-deul-e-ge al-lip-ni-da.]
소방관이 도착 할 때까지, 침착해야 합니다.
Until the firefighters arrive, you have to be calm.
[so-bang-gwan-i do-chak hal ttae-kka-ji, chim-chak-hae-ya hap-ni-da.]
매년 약 오백명의 사람이 화재로 사망합니다.
Every year about five million people die of fire.
[mae-nyeon yak o-baek-myeong-ui sa-ram-i hwa-jae-ro sa-mang-hap-ni-da.]
교통사고보다 많은 숫자입니다.
It's a number greater than car accidents.
[gyo-tong-sa-go-bo-da man-eun sut-ja-ip-ni-da.]
모든 사고는 예방할 수 있습니다.
Every accident can be prevented.
[mo-deun sa-go-neun ye-bang-hal su it-seup-ni-da.]
만약을 대비해, 집에 소화기를 사 놓아야 합니다.
To be prepared for the unforeseen, you need to buy an extinguisher for your home.
[man-yak-eul dae-bi-hae, jip-e so-hwa-gi-reul sa no-a-ya hap-ni-da.]
그리고, 비상구가 어디 있는지 기억해야 합니다.
And, you have to remember where the emergency exit is.
[geu-ri-go, bi-sang-gu-ga eo-di it-neun-ji gi-eok-hae-ya hap-ni-da.]

Answer Keys : (1) 2 (2) 2 (3) 3 (4) 5 (5) 4 (6) 3 (7) 2 (8) 3
(9) 1 (10) 1 (11) 4 (12) 1

Practice #35

여행을 할 때는 소지품을 분실하는 경우가 많습니다.
When traveling, losing one's belongings happens often.
[yeo-haeng-eul hal ttae-neun so-ji-pum-eul bun-shil-ha-neun gyeong-u-ga man-seup-ni-da.]
설문조사에 따르면, 지갑을 가장 많이 잃어버린다고 합니다.
According to a survey, wallets are lost the most.
[seol-mun-jo-sa-e tta-reu-myeon, ji-gap-eul ga-jang man-i il-eo-beo-rin-da-go hap-ni-da.]
주로 관광지에서 소매치기를 당한다고 합니다.
It's said that they are mostly pickpocketed at tourist spots.
[ju-ro gwan-gwang-ji-e-seo so-mae-chi-gi-reul dang-han-da-go hap-ni-da.]
외국에서는 언어가 통하지 않아서 문제 해결이 쉽지 않습니다.
In foreign countries, resolving an issue is not easy due to the language barrier.
[oe-guk-e-seo-neun eon-eo-ga tong-ha-ji an-a-seo mun-je hae-gyeol-i ship-ji an-seup-ni-da.]
경찰서에 가도 큰 도움이 되지 않습니다.
Going to the police station isn't a big help.
[gyeong-chal-seo-e ga-do keun do-um-i doe-ji an-seup-ni-da.]
그래서 지갑은 옷의 안쪽 주머니에 넣는것이 좋습니다.
So it's good to keep the wallet in a pocket on the inner side of the clothes.
[geu-rae-seo ji-gap-eun o-sui an-jjok ju-meo-ni-e neot-neun geo-shi jot-seup-ni-da.]
돈을 한번에 모두 가지고 다니는 것도 좋지 않습니다.
It's also not good to carry a large amount of money at once.
[don-eul han-beon-e mo-du ga-ji-go da-ni-neun geot-do jot-chi an-seup-ni-da.]
큰 돈은 호텔 금고에 보관해야 합니다.
A large amount of money must be kept in a hotel safe.
[keun don-eun ho-tel geum-go-e bo-gwan-hae-ya hap-ni-da.]
여권을 잃어버리면, 영사관에 가야합니다.
If you lose your passport, you need to go to the embassy.
[yeo-gwon-eul il-eo-beo-ri-myeon, yeong-sa-gwan-e ga-ya-hap-ni-da.]
여권을 다시 만들려면 보통 일주일 정도 시간이 걸립니다.
It usually takes about a week to have your passport made.
[yeo-gwon-eul da-shi man-deul-lyeo-myeon bo-tong il-ju-il jeong-do shi-gan-i geol-lip-ni-da.]
하지만 특수한 경우에는 당일에도 만들 수 있습니다.
But in special cases, it can be made the same day.
[ha-ji-man teuk-su-han gyeong-u-e-neun dang-il-e-do man-deul su it-seup-ni-da.]
여행자 보험을 듣는 것은 필수입니다.
Getting traveler's insurance is a must.
[yeo-haeng-ja bo-heom-eul deut-neun geo-seun pil-su-ip-ni-da.]

Answer Keys : (1) 5 (2) 2 (3) 1 (4) 4 (5) 2 (6) 1 (7) 2 (8) 2
(9) 5 (10) 3 (11) 2 (12) 1

Practice #36

노래를 부르는 것은 건강에 이롭습니다.
Singing is beneficial for health.
[no-rae-reul bu-reu-neun geo-seun geon-gang-e i-rop-seun-ni-da.]
심리적으로도 그렇고, 육체적으로도 그렇습니다.
Both psychologically, and physically so.
[shim-li-jeok-eu-ro-do geu-reot-go, yuk-che-jeok-eu-ro-do geu-reot-seup-ni-da.]
노래를 부르면, 혈액순환이 활발해집니다.
If you sing, blood circulation becomes active.
[no-rae-reul bu-reu-myeon, hyeol-aek-sun-hwan-i hwal-bal-hae-jip-ni-da.]
행복을 느끼는 호르몬도 나옵니다.
It releases hormones that feel happiness.
[haeng-bok-eul neu-kki-neun ho-reu-mon-do na-op-ni-da.]
큰 소리로 노래를 부르면, 효과가 더욱 좋습니다.
If you sing a song with a loud voice, it's more effective.
[keun so-ri-ro no-rae-reul bu-reu-myeon, hyo-gwa-ga deo-uk jot-seup-ni-da.]
연구에 따르면, 동물들도 노래를 부를 수 있다고 합니다.
According to research, animals can sing too.
[yeon-gu-e tta-reu-myeon, dong-mul-deul-do no-rae-reul bu-reul su it-da-go hap-ni-da.]
기분이 좋을때와 나쁠때, 목소리가 다릅니다.
Their voices are different when they are in a good mood and bad mood.
[gi-bun-i jo-eul-ttae-wa na-bbeul-ttae, mok-so-ri-ga da-reup-ni-da.]
그리고, 뇌의 반응도 다릅니다.
Also, the brain's reactions are different.
[geu-ri-go, noe-ui ban-eung-do da-reup-ni-da.]
이 것은, 과학이 발전했기 때문에 가능한 것입니다.
This is possible because of the advancement of science.
[i geo-seun, gwa-hak-i bal-jeon-haet-gi ttae-mun-e ga-neung-han geo-ship-ni-da.]
예전에는, 동물에게는 감정이 없다고 생각했습니다.
Before, it used to be thought that animals don't have emotions.
[ye-jeon-e-neun, dong-mul-e-ge-neun gam-jeong-i eop-da-go saeng-gak-haet-seup-ni-da.]
이제는, 동물의 언어를 분석하기 위해 연구 중입니다.
Now, (we are) researching to analyze the languages of animals.
[i-je-neun, dong-mul-ui eon-eo-reul bun-seok-ha-gi wi-hae yeon-gu-jung-ip-ni-da.]
십년 안에, 동물과 인간은 대화를 나눌 수 있을 것입니다.
Within ten years, animals and humans would be able to exchange a conversation.
[ship-nyeon an-e, dong-mul-gwa in-gan-eun dae-hwa-reul na-nul su it-seul geo-ship-ni-da.]

Answer Keys : (1) 4 (2) 1 (3) 2 (4) 4 (5) 1 (6) 1 (7) 1 (8) 2
(9) 2 (10) 2 (11) 1 (12) 2

Practice #37

인구 중 절반 이상이 아침 식사를 하지 못한다고 합니
다. More than half of the population can't have breakfast.
[in-gu jung jeol-ban i-sang-i a-chim shik-sa-reul ha-ji mot-
han-da-go hap-ni-da.]
아침 식사는 하루 중 가장 중요한 식사입니다.
Breakfast is the most important meal of the day.
[a-chim shik-sa-neun ha-ru jung ga-jang jung-yo-han shik-
sa-ip-ni-da.]
우리의 뇌가 깨어나는 시간이기 때문입니다.
Because it's the time our brains wake up.
[u-ri-ui noe-ga kkae-eo-na-neun shi-gan-i-gi ttae-mun-ip-ni-
da.]
실제로, 아침 식사를 하는 학생들의 성적이 더욱 좋습
니다. Actually, the students who have breakfast get better
grades.
[shil-je-ro, a-chim shik-sa-reul ha-neun hak-saeng-deul-ui
seong-jeok-i deo-uk jot-seup-ni-da.]
그 중에서도 수학 성적이 차이가 많이 납니다.
Among all, math grades have the largest differences.
[geu jung-e-seo-do su-hak seong-jeok-i cha-i-ga man-i nap-
ni-da.]
조금이라도 아침 식사를 하는 것이, 하지 않는 것 보다
좋습니다.
Having at least a little bit of breakfast is better than not
having it.
[jo-geum-i-ra-do a-chim shik-sa-reul ha-neun geo-shi, ha-ji
an-neun geot bo-da jot-seup-ni-da.]
우유 한 잔을 마셔도 큰 도움이 됩니다.
Drinking a glass of milk is a big help, too.
[u-yu han jan-eul ma-shyeo-do keun do-um-i doep-ni-da.]
하지만 아침을 너무 많이 먹으면, 잠이 오게 될 수 있
습니다.
But if you have breakfast too much, it might make you
sleepy.
[ha-ji-man, a-chim-eul neo-mu man-i meok-eu-myeon,
jam-i o-ge doel su it-seup-ni-da.]
아침 식사를 하지 못하면, 점심을 많이 먹게 될 수 있
습니다.
If you can't have breakfast, you might eat lunch a lot.
[a-chim shik-sa-reul ha-ji mot-ha-myeon, jeom-shim-eul
man-i meok-ge doel su it-seup-ni-da.]
이것은 비만의 원인이 될 수 있습니다.
This might be a reason for obesity.
[i-geo-seun bi-man-ui won-in-i doel su it-seup-ni-da.]
하루 전 날 저녁, 다음날 아침 식사를 미리 만드는 것
도 좋습니다.
It's good to make the next day's breakfast in advance the
night before.
[ha-ru jeon nal jeo-nyeok, da-eum-nal a-chim shik-sa-reul
mi-ri man-deu-neun geot-do jot-seup-ni-da.]
아침에 바쁜 사람들에게 특히 그렇습니다.
Especially so for those who are busy in the morning.
[a-chim-e ba-bbeun sa-ram-deul-e-ge teuk-hi geu-reot-seup-
ni-da.]

Answer Keys : (1) 3 (2) 1 (3) 3 (4) 2 (5) 3 (6) 2 (7) 1 (8) 5
(9) 1 (10) 3 (11) 3 (12) 3

Practice #38

한국의 예절은 생각보다 복잡합니다.
Manners in Korea are more complicated than you think.
[han-guk-ui ye-jeol-eun saeng-gak-bo-da bok-jap-hap-ni-da.]
특히 어른들과 술을 마실 때에는 신경을 써야합니다.
Especially, you have to pay attention when you drink with older
people.
[teuk-hi eo-reun-deul-gwa sul-eul ma-shil ttae-e-neun shin-gyeong-
eul sseo-ya-hap-ni-da.]
의도와는 다르게, 예의 없는 사람으로 보일 수 있습니다.
Different from your intention, you might be viewed as a
mannerless person.
[ui-do-wa-neun da-reu-ge, ye-ui eop-neun sa-ram-eu-ro bo-il su
it-seup-ni-da.]
어른께 술을 따라드릴 때에는, 두 손으로 해야 합니다.
When pouring alcohol to older people, you have to use two hands.
[eo-reun-kke sul-eul tta-ra-deu-ril ttae-e-neun, du son-eu-ro hae-ya
hap-ni-da.]
어른으로부터 술을 받을때도, 두 손을 사용해야 합니다.
When receiving alcohol from older people, you have do use two
hands.
[eo-reun-eu-ro-bu-teo sul-eul bat-eul ttae-do, du son-eul sa-yong-
hae-ya hap-ni-da.]
하지만 외국인이 실수하면, 너그럽게 용서합니다.
But if a foreigner makes a mistake, it's generously forgiven.
[ha-ji-man oe-guk-in-i shil-su-ha-myeon, neo-geu-reop-ge yong-
seo-hap-ni-da.]
한국어의 존댓말 또한 굉장히 복잡합니다.
The honorifics of Korean are very complicated too.
[han-guk-eo-ui jon-daet-mal tto-han goeng-jang-hi bok-jap-hap-ni-
da.]
어른들과 친구에게 사용하는 단어가 다릅니다.
The words you use to older people and friends are different.
[eo-reun-deul-gwa chin-gu-e-ge sa-yong-ha-neun dan-eo-ga da-
reup-ni-da.]
한국인들도 가끔씩 틀릴 때가 있습니다.
Even Koreans often get it wrong.
[han-guk-in-deul-do ga-kkeum-ssik teul-lil ttae-ga it-seup-ni-da.]
특히 드라마나 영화에서도 틀리게 쓰이는 것을 볼 수 있습니
다.
Especially in dramas and movies, you can see them being used
incorrectly.
[teuk-hi deu-ra-ma-na yeong-hwa-e-seo-do teul-li-ge sseu-i-neun
geo-seul bol su it-seup-ni-da.]
하지만 진짜 예의는 마음에서 나옵니다.
But real manners come from the heart.
[ha-ji-man jin-jja ye-ui-neun ma-eum-e-seo na-op-ni-da.]
어려서부터 타인을 존중하는 교육을 해야합니다.
You have to educate them to respect others since they are little.
[eo-ryeo-seo-bu-teo ta-in-eul jon-jung-ha-neun gyo-yuk-eul hae-
ya-hap-ni-da.]

Answer Keys : (1) 2 (2) 1 (3) 1 (4) 1 (5) 2 (6) 2 (7) 2 (8) 1
(9) 2 (10) 1 (11) 3 (12) 1

Practice #39

축구는 세계에서 가장 인기있는 종목입니다.
Soccer is the most popular sport in the world.
[chuk-gu-neun se-gye-e-seo ga-jang in-gi-it-neun jong-mok-ip-ni-da.]
남녀노소 관계 없이, 누구나 좋아합니다.
Regardless of age and sex, everybody likes it.
[nam-nyeo-no-so gwan-gye eop-shi, nu-gu-na jo-a-hap-ni-da.]
규칙이 간단한 것이 가장 큰 인기 이유입니다.
Rules being simple is the biggest reason for popularity.
[gyu-chik-i gan-dan-han geo-shi ga-jang keun in-gi i-yu-ip-ni-da.]
공만 있으면 즐길 수 있습니다.
You can enjoy it if there is just a ball.
[gong-man it-seu-myeon jeul-gil su it-seup-ni-da.]
간단한 규칙과는 다르게, 다양한 기술이 필요합니다.
Unlike simple rules, various skills are needed.
[gan-dan-han gy-chik-gwa-neun da-reu-ge, da-yang-han gi-sul-i pil-yo-hap-ni-da.]
빠르게 달리기는 무엇보다 중요합니다.
Running fast is more important than any other.
[bba-reu-ge dal-li-gi-neun mu-eot-bo-da jung-yo-hap-ni-da.]
정확하게 공을 발로 차는 능력도 필요합니다.
Kicking the ball accurately is also necessary.
[jeong-hwak-ha-ge gong-eul bal-lo cha-neun neung-ryeok-do pil-yo-hap-ni-da.]
쉬지 않고 달릴 수 있는 지구력도 필요합니다.
Endurance to run without stopping is also necessary.
[shwi-ji an-ko dal-lil su it-neun ji-gu-ryeok-do pil-yo-hap-ni-da.]
모두 연습을 통해 발달 시킬 수 있습니다.
They all can be developed through practice.
[mo-du yeon-seup-eul tong-hae bal-dal shi-kil su it-seup-ni-da.]
하지만 누구나 똑같은 재능을 갖고 있지 않습니다.
But not everybody has the same talent.
[ha-ji-man nu-gu-na ttok-gat-eun jae-neung-eul gat-go it-ji an-seup-ni-da.]
그래서 각각 다른 역할을 맡아야 합니다.
So each has to assume different roles.
[geu-rae-seo gak-gak da-reun yeok-hal-eul mat-a-ya hap-ni-da.]
수비와 공격으로 나누어 연습합니다.
They practice, divided into defense and offense.
[su-bi-wa gong-gyeok-eu-ro na-nu-eo yeon-seup-hap-ni-da.]

Answer Keys : (1) 5 (2) 2 (3) 3 (4) 2 (5) 2 (6) 1 (7) 2 (8) 4
(9) 2 (10) 2 (11) 4 (12) 1

태권도는 매우 세계적인 무예입니다.
Taekwondo is a very international martial art.
[tae-kwon-do-neun mae-u se-gye-jeok-in mu-ye-ip-ni-da.]
팔천만명이 넘는 사람들이 배우고 있습니다.
Over eighty million people are learning it.
[pal-cheon-man-myeong-i neom-neun sa-ram-deul-i bae-u-go it-seup-ni-da.]
손과 발을 주로 쓰지만, 발을 더욱 많이 사용합니다. Hand and foot are mainly used, but the foot is used more.
[son-gwa bal-eul ju-ro sseu-ji-man, bal-eul deo-uk man-i sa-yong-hap-ni-da]
태권도는 타인을 공격하는 것이 목적이 아닙니다.
Taekwondo's purpose is not to attack other people.
[tae-kwon-do-neun ta-in-eul gong-gyeok-han-neun geo-shi mok-jeok-i a-nip-ni-da.]
자신의 마음을 단련하는 것이 목표입니다.
Training one's mind is the purpose.
[ja-shin-ui ma-eum-eul dan-ryeon-ha-neun geo-shi mok-pyo-ip-ni-da.]
그렇게 하면, 몸과 마음 모두 건강해 질 수 있습니다.
If done so, your body and mind both can be healthy.
[geu-reot-ge ha-myeon, mom-gwa ma-eum mo-du geon-gang-hae jil su it-seup-ni-da.]
태권도는 올림픽 정식 종목입니다.
Taekwondo is an official sport of the Olympics.
[tae-kwon-do-neun ol-lim-pik jeong-shik jong-mok-ip-ni-da.]
요즘에는 외국 선수들도 일등을 많이 합니다. Nowadays foreign players win first place a lot.
[yo-jeum-e-neun oe-guk seon-su-deul-do il-deung-eul man-i hap-ni-da.]
한국의 태권도 선생님이 외국에서 학생들을 많이 가르치기 때문입니다.
It's because Korean Taekwondo instructors teach students overseas a lot.
[han-guk-ui tae-kwon-do seon-saeng-nim-i oe-guk-e-seo hak-saeng-deul-eul man-i ga-reu-chi-gi ttae-mun-ip-ni-da.]
태권도를 배우고, 한국에 대한 관심이 생긴 외국인들이 많습니다.
After learning Taekwondo, there are a lot of foreigners who became interested in Korea.
[tae-kwon-do-reul bae-u-go, han-guk-e dae-han gwan-shim-i saeng-gin oe-guk-in-deul-i man-seup-ni-da.]
그들은 직접 한국을 방문해 태권도의 역사를 공부합니다.
They visit Korea in person and study the history of Taekwondo.
[geu-deul-eun jik-jeop han-guk-eul bang-mun-hae tae-kwon-do-ui yeok-sa-reul gong-bu-hap-ni-da.]
태권도는 한국의 자랑스러운 수출품 입니다.
Taekwondo is Korea's proud export.
[tae-kwon-do-neun han-guk-ui ja-rang-seu-reo-un su-chul-pum ip-ni-da.]

Answer Keys : (1) 2 (2) 4 (3) 2 (4) 2 (5) 1 (6) 3 (7) 2 (8) 1
(9) 2 (10) 1 (11) 2 (12) 2

Practice #40

Read the following passage carefully and answer the following questions.

언어를 배우는 데 있어서 가장 효과적인 방법은 모방이라고 한다.
[eon-eo-reul bae-u-neun de it-seo-seo ga-jang hyo-gwa-jeok-in bang-beop-eun mo-bang-i-ra-go han-da.]

실제로, 어린 아기들은 부모가 말하는 법을 보고 배운다.
[shil-je-ro, eo-rin a-gi-deul-eun bu-mo-ga mal-ha-neun beop-eul bo-go bae-un-da.]

심지어, 사소한 습관까지 그대로 따라한다.
[shim-ji-eo, sa-so-han seup-gwan-kka-ji geu-dae-ro tta-ra-han-da.]

몸짓과 표정을 통해 감정을 전달하는 방법도 익힌다.
[mom-jit-gwa pyo-jeong-eul tong-hae gam-jeong-eul jeon-dal-ha-neun bang-beop-do ik-hin-da.]

흥미로운 사실은, 동물들도 모방을 통해 언어를 배운다는 것이다.
[heung-mi-ro-un sa-shil-eun, dong-mul-deul-do mo-bang-eul tong-hae eon-eo-reul bae-un-da-neun geo-shi-da.]

예를들어, 아기 강아지들은 부모가 짖는 소리를 똑같이 흉내낸다.
[ye-reul-deul-eo, a-gi gang-a-ji-deul-eun bu-mo-ga jit-neun so-ri-reul ttok-ga-chi hyung-nae-naen-da.]

언어학자들에 따르면, 태어나서 십 년 동안이 가장 중요한 시기라고 한다.
[eon-eo-hak-ja-deul-e tta-reu-myeon, tae-eo-na-seo ship nyeon dong-an-i ga-jang jung-yo-han shi-gi-ra-go han-da.]

이 시기가 지나면, 새로운 언어를 배우는 것이 힘들다고 한다.
[i shi-gi-ga ji-na-myeon, sae-ro-un eon-eo-reul bae-u-neun geo-shi him-deul-da-go han-da.]

따라서, 어렸을때 받는 교육이 매우 중요하다.
[tta-ra-seo, eo-reyot-sseul-ttae bat-neun gyo-yuk-i mae-u jung-yo-ha-da.]

세계에는 약 백개가 넘는 언어가 존재한다.
[se-gye-e-neun yak baek-gae-ga neom-neun eon-eo-ga jon-jae-han-da.]

그 중에서 가장 많은 사람들이 사용하는 언어는 중국어다.
[geu jung-e-seo ga-jang man-eun sa-ram-deul-i sa-yong-ha-neun eon-eo-neun jung-guk-eo-da.]

기술이 발달하면, 언어를 배우는 것이 필요 없게 될 전망이다.
[gi-sul-i bal-dal-ha-myeon, eon-eo-reul bae-u-neun geo-shi pil-yo eop-ge doel jeon-mang-i-da.]

Question 1. According to the passage, the most effective method of learning a language is...

1. Questioning 2. Reasoning 3. Listening 4. Imitating 5. Singing

Question 2. According to the passage, who do babies learn how to talk from?

1. Teachers 2. Friends 3. Cartoon Characters 4. Other Babies 5. Parents

Question 3. According to the passage, babies also imitate...

1. Little Habits 2. Nuances 3. Pronunciation 4. Accent 5. Grammar

Question 4. According to the passage, babies also learn to express emotions through...

1. Gesture and Facial Expressions 2. Speed and Pitch 3. Accent and Pronunciation 4. Sign Language

Question 5. True or False...? Animals learn a language in a way different from that of humans.

1. True 2. False

Question 6. According to the passage, baby puppies can imitate the barking sound of their...

1. Siblings 2. Predators 3. Masters 4. Parents 5. Surroundings

Question 7. According to WHO is the ten-year period from birth is the most important period?

1. Association of Sign Language 2. Linguists 3. Professors 4. Parents 5. Pediatrician

Question 8. True or False...? After that period, it's difficult to learn a new language.

1. True 2. False

Question 9. True or False...? According to the author, for learning a new language, timing doesn't really matter if it's done properly.

1. True 2. False

Question 10. According to the passage, how many languages are there in the world?

1. Around 10 2. Less Than 50 3. More Than 80 4. About 90 5. About Over 100

Question 11. True or False...? Chinese is the most used language in the world.

1. True 2. False

Question 12. According to the passage, learning a new language might not be necessary with...

1. Government Funding 2. New Language Programs 3. Technological Advancement 4. Smart Devices

Read the following passage carefully and answer the following questions.

운전을 할 때는 고도의 집중력이 필요하다.
[un-jeon-eul hal ttae-neun go-do-ui jip-jung-ryeok-i pil-yo-ha-da.]

음악을 들으면서 운전을 하는 것 도 위험하다.
[eum-ak-eul deul-eu-myeon-seo un-jeon-eul ha-neun geot do wi-heom-ha-da.]

한국은 교통 사고 사망률이 높은 편이다.
[han-guk-eun gyo-tong sa-go sa-mang-ryul-i nop-eun pyeon-i-da.]

무엇보다 고령 운전자들의 사고가 많다.
[mu-eot-bo-da go-ryeong un-jeon-ja-deul-ui sa-go-ga man-ta.]

이러한 이유에서, 팔십 세 이상의 운전은 권장되지 않는다.
[i-reo-han i-yu-e-seo, pal-ship se i-sang-ui un-jeon-eun gwon-jang-doe-ji an-neun-da.]

그대신, 그들은 무료로 대중교통을 사용할 수 있다.
[geu-dae-shin, geu-deul-eun mu-ryo-ro dae-jung-gyo-tong-eul sa-yong-hal su it-da.]

미래에는, 사람이 직접 운전하지 않아도 되는 시대가 올 것이다.
[mi-rae-e-neun, sa-ram-i jik-jeop un-jeon-ha-ji an-a-do doe-neun shi-dae-ga ol geo-shi-da.]

과학자들이 열심히 연구하고 있지만, 아직 완벽하지 않다.
[gwa-hak-ja-deul-i yeol-shim-hi yeon-gu-ha-go it-ji-man, a-jik wan-byeok-ha-ji an-ta.]

앞으로 많은 시행착오를 겪어야 할 것이다.
[ap-eu-ro man-eun shi-haeng-chak-o-reul gyeok-eo-ya hal geo-shi-da.]

그리고, 자동차를 소유하는 것이 필요 없게 될 것이다.
[geu-ri-go, ja-dong-cha-reul so-yu-ha-neun geo-shi pil-yo eop-ge doel geo-shi-da.]

하늘을 나는 자동차도 등장 할 것이다.
[ha-neul-eul na-neun ja-dong-cha-do deung-jang hal geo-shi-da.]

이 모든 것은 공상과학 영화 속의 이야기가 아니다.
[i mo-deun geo-seun gong-sang-gwa-hak yeong-hwa sok-ui i-ya-gi-ga a-ni-da.]

Question 1. According to the passage, you need a high level of THIS when you drive.

1. Concentration 2. Passion 3. Tenacity 4. Determination 5. Assistance

Question 2. According to the passage, doing THIS while driving is dangerous.

1. Watching DVD 2. Reading a Book 3. Looking at Smartphone 4. Listening to Music 5. Eating Snacks

Question 3. True or False...? Compared to other countries, the death rate from car accidents in Korea is low.

1. True 2. False

Question 4. According to the passage, who makes up a large portion of such accidents?

1. Teenagers 2. Drivers Without License 3. Uninsured Drivers 4. Female Drivers 5. Elderly Drivers

Question 5. True or False...? Drivers over the age of 80 are not allowed to drive.

1. True 2. False

Question 6. True or False...? Drivers over the age of 80 can use public transportation at a discounted price.

1. True 2. False

Question 7. According to the passage, people won't have to...

1. Drive Their Cars 2. Fuel Their Cars 3. Change Flat Tires 4. Buy a Car 5. Maintain Their Cars

Question 8. True or False...? Cars being researched by scientists with the technology mentioned above are nearly perfect now.

1. True 2. False

Question 9. According to the passage, cars mentioned above will have to go through a lot of...?

1. Tests 2. Trial and Error 3. Criticism 4. Accidents 5. Planning

Question 10. According to the passage, what won't be necessary in the future?

1. Owning a Car 2. Hailing a Cab 3. Taking the Public Transportation 4. Tires 5. Fuel

Question 11. According to the passage, what will appear in the near future?

1. Flying Cars 2. Underground Cars 3. Teleporter 4. Personal Helicopter 5. Super Drones

Question 12. True or False...? Everything mentioned in the passage is stories from a sci-fi movie.

1. True 2. False

Read the following passage carefully and answer the following questions.

한국은 지금 남과 북으로 나뉘어져 있습니다.
[han-guk-eun ji-geum nam-gwa buk-eu-ro na-nwi-eo-jyeo it-seup-ni-da]

반 세기 전 있었던 전쟁 때문입니다.
[ban se-gi jeon it-seot-deon jeon-jaeng ttae-mun-ip-ni-da.]

같은 민족이지만, 다른 이념으로 인해 싸웠습니다.
[ga-teun min-jok-i-ji-man, da-reum i-nyeom-eu-ro in-hae ssa-wot-seup-ni-da.]

대부분의 사람들은 고향을 떠났습니다.
[dae-bu-bun-ui sa-ram-deul-eun go-hyang-eul tteo-nat-seup-ni-da.]

그리고, 가족들과 헤어져야 했습니다.
[geu-ri-go, ga-jok-deul-gwa he-eo-jyeo-ya haet-seup-ni-da.]

정치인들은 문제를 해결하기 위해 노력하고 있습니다.
[jeong-chi-in-deul-eun mun-je-reul hae-gyeol-ha-gi wi-hae no-ryeok-ha-go it-seup-ni-da.]

하지만 통일이 되려면 시간이 많이 필요합니다.
[ha-ji-man tong-il-i doe-ryeo-myeon shi-gan-i man-i pil-yo-hap-ni-da.]

다행히도, 남과 북은 같은 언어를 사용합니다.
[da-haeng-hi-do, nam-gwa buk-eun ga-teun eon-eo-reul sa-yong-hap-ni-da.]

하지만 문화는 많이 차이가 납니다.
[ha-ji-man mun-hwa-neun man-i cha-i-ga nap-ni-da.]

경제력도 큰 격차가 생겼습니다.
[mo-deun sa-go-neun ye-bang-hal su it-seup-ni-da.]

만약 남과 북이 합쳐지면, 단점보다는 장점이 많아질 것 입니다.
[man-yak-eul dae-bi-hae, jip-e so-hwa-gi-reul sa no-a-ya hap-ni-da.]

여행 갈 수 있는 곳도 더욱 많아지겠죠.
[geu-ri-go, bi-sang-gu-ga eo-di it-neun-ji gi-eok-hae-ya hap-ni-da.]

Question 1. True or False...? Korea is divided between West and East.

1. True 2. False

Question 2. According to the passage, it's because of a war that took place three centuries ago.

1. True 2. False

Question 3. According to the passage, they fought because of THIS despite they are of the same nationality.

1. History 2. Culture 3. Politics 4. Ideology 5. Territory

Question 4. True or False...? Most of the people decided not to leave their hometowns during the war.

1. True 2. False

Question 5. True or False...? Families didn't have to separate because they all stayed together.

1. True 2. False

Question 6. According to the passage, who is working to solve the problem?

1. United Nations 2. Politicians 3. Scholars 4. Historians 5. Everybody

Question 7. True or False...? It shouldn't need a lot of time for unification to happen.

1. True 2. False

Question 8. According to the passage, North and South use the same...

1. Currency 2. Language 3. Metric System 4. Textbooks 5. Government System

Question 9. According to the passage, there is a big difference between their...

1. Languages 2. Currencies 3. Textbooks 4. Government Systems 5. Cultures

Question 10. True or False...? Their economic powers are about the same level.

1. True 2. False

Question 11. True of False...? Unification will cause more troubles than benefits.

1. True 2. False

Question 12. According to the passage, there will be more places to do THIS when unified.

1. Construct New Buildings 2. Farm 3. Travel 4. Conquer 5. Develop

Practice #44 (Difficulty ★★★★★)

Read the following passage carefully and answer the following questions.

감기에 걸리는 이유는 우리가 생각하는 것 보다 많습니다.
[gam-gi-e geol-li-neun i-yu-neun u-ri-ga saeng-gak-ha-neun geot bo-da man-seup-ni-da.]

그리고, 상식과 다른 것도 많습니다.
[geu-ri-go, sang-sik-gwa da-reun geot-do man-seup-ni-da.]

예를들어, 우리는 추운 곳에서 감기가 더 잘 걸린다고 생각합니다.
[ye-reul-deul-eo, u-ri-neun chu-un go-se-seo gam-gi-ga deo jal geol-lin-da-go saeng-gak-hap-ni-da.]

하지만 오히려 추운 곳에서는 감기 균이 활동하지 못한다고 합니다.
[ha-ji-man o-hi-yreo chu-un go-se-seo-neun gam-gi gyun-i hwal-dong-ha-ji mot-han-da-go hap-ni-da.]

기온의 차이가 크게 날 때 감기에 더 잘 걸립니다.
[gi-on-ui cha-i-ga keu-ge nal ttae gam-gi-e deo jal geol-lip-ni-da.]

우리 몸의 면역체계가 변화에 대처하지 못하기 때문입니다.
[u-ri mom-ui myeon-yeok-che-gye-ga byeon-hwa-e dae-cheo-ha-ji mot-ha-gi ttae-mun-ip-ni-da.]

그래서, 항상 여분의 옷을 가지고 다니는 것이 권장됩니다.
[geu-rae-seo, hang-sang yeo-bun-ui o-seul ga-ji-go da-ni-neun geo-shi gwon-jang-doep-ni-da.]

감기에 걸리면, 목을 따뜻하게 하는 것이 효과적입니다.
[gam-gi-e geol-li-myeon, mok-eul tta-tteut-ha-ge ha-neun geo-shi hyo-gwa-jeok-ip-ni-da.]

목도리를 하는 것이 가장 쉬운 방법입니다.
[mok-do-ri-reul ha-neun geo-shi ga-jang shwi-un bang-beop-ip-ni-da.]

술을 마시는 것은 피해야 합니다.
[sul-eul ma-shi-neun geo-seun pi-hae-ya hap-ni-da.]

탈수로 인해 몸의 저항력이 떨어지기 때문입니다.
[tal-su-ro in-hae mom-ui jeo-hang-ryeok-i tteol-eo-ji-gi ttae-mun-ip-ni-da.]

하지만 따뜻한 포도주를 마시는 것이 전통인 나라도 있습니다.
[ha-ji-man tta-tteut-han po-do-ju-reul ma-shi-neun geo-shi jeon-tong-in na-ra-do it-seup-ni-da.]

Question 1. True or False...? There are more reasons for catching a cold than we think.

1. True 2. False

Question 2. According to the passage, there are many reasons that are different from our...

1. Belief 2. Experience 3. Common Knowledge 4. Lessons 5. Analysis

Question 3. As an example for the above, we think that we catch a cold more easily in...

1. Dirty Places 2. Humid Places 3. Cold Places 4. Sterile Place 5. Foreign Place

Question 4. True or False..? cold viruses are less active in cold places.

1. True 2. False

Question 5. According to the passage, we catch a cold more easily when...

1. Weather is Unpredictable 2. Temperature Difference is Big 3. People Are More Active
4. Outside 5. Jetlagged

Question 6. According to the passage, the reason for the above is because...

1. Our Sensory Organs Become Less Sensitive 2. Our Immune System Can't Cope With Changes
3. Our Hormones Get More Active 4. Our Body Becomes Cold

Question 7. For the reason mentioned above, it's recommended that you always carry a/an...

1. Extra Clothing 2. Cold Medicine 3. Tumbler 4. Mask 5. Sanitizer

Question 8. According to the passage, what's effective when you have a cold?

1. Taking a Bath 2. Drinking Salt Water 3. Keeping Your Neck Warm 4. Putting on a Hat 5. Sleep

Question 9. According to the passage, what's the easiest way for the above mentioned?

1. Putting on a Hat 2. Taking a Sleeping Pill 3. Drinking Hot Coffee 4. Putting on a Scarf 5. Bathing

Question 10. According to the passage, what should you avoid doing?

1. Taking Too Much Salt 2. Drinking Too Much Water 3. Washing Hands Too Often 4. Drinking Alcohol

Question 11. According to the passage, doing what's mentioned above weakens your immune system because it makes your body...

1. Shrink 2. Swell Up 3. Dehydrated 4. Exhausted 5. Vulnerable

Question 12. True or False...? In some countries, drinking THIS is a tradition.

1. Cold Beer 2. Warm Whiskey 3. Warm Wine 4. Hot Chocolate 5. Sugar Water

Read the following passage carefully and answer the following questions.

한반도는 자연재해가 많지 않은 편입니다.
[han-ban-do-neun ja-yeon-jae-hae-ga man-chi an-eun pyeon-ip-ni-da.]

하지만 태풍은 아주 파괴력이 큽니다.
[ha-ji-man tae-pung-eun a-ju pa-goe-ryeok-i keup-ni-da.]

태풍이 오면 엄청난 양의 비가 내리고, 강한 바람이 붑니다.
[tae-pung-i o-myeon eom-cheong-nan yang-ui bi-ga nae-ri-go, gang-han ba-ram-i bup-ni-da.]

차량의 운행이 금지 될 정도입니다.
[cha-ryang-ui un-haeng-i geum-ji doel jeong-do-ip-ni-da.]

하지만 가장 큰 피해를 보는 곳은 농촌입니다.
[ha-ji-man ga-jang keun pi-hae-reul bo-neun go-seun nong-chon-ip-ni-da.]

과일이 나무에서 떨어지고, 상처가 납니다.
[gwa-il-i na-mu-e-seo tteol-eo-ji-go, sang-cheo-ga nap-ni-da.]

반대로, 비가 너무 오지 않아서 문제가 되기도 합니다.
[ban-dae-ro, bi-ga neo-mu o-ji an-a-seo mun-je-ga doe-gi-do hap-ni-da.]

가뭄이 찾아오면, 사람이 할 수 있는 것은 별로 없습니다.
[ga-mum-i cha-ja-o-myeon, sa-ram-i hal su it-neun geo-seun byeol-lo eop-seup-ni-da.]

비가 오기만을 기다릴 수 밖에 없습니다.
[bi-ga o-gi-man-eul gi-da-ril su bak-e eop-seup-ni-da.]

가뭄이 심한 해에는, 과일 값이 폭등합니다.
[ga-mum-i shim-han ttae-e-neun gwa-il gap-shi pok-deung-hap-ni-da.]

그래서 과일을 수입해서 가격을 안정시키기도 합니다.
[geu-rae-seo gwa-il-eul su-ip-hae-seo ga-gyeok-eul an-jeong-shi-ki-gi-do hap-ni-da.]

한국에서 가장 많이 소비되는 과일은 사과입니다.
[han-gul-e-seo ga-jang man-i so-bi-doe-neun gwa-il-eun sa-gwa-ip-ni-da.]

Question 1. According to the passage, the Korean peninsula doesn't have many...

1. Accidents 2. Deaths 3. Natural Disasters 4. Environmental Issues 5. Human Right Issues

Question 2. According to the passage, hurricanes are...

1. Highly Dangerous 2. Hugely Destructive 3. Relatively Weak 4. As Powerful As Thunderstorms

Question 3. According to the passage, when a hurricane hits, it...

1. Only Rains A Lot 2. Only Has Strong Winds 3. Rains and Hails 4. Rains A Lot and Has Strong Winds

Question 4. According to the passage, as a result of the above...

1. Driving Is Not Allowed 2. Public Transportation Is Interrupted 3. Schools Are Closed
4. Government Is Temporarily Shut Down 5. Emergency Exits Are Automatically Opened

Question 5. According to the passage, the place that gets the most damage is...

1. Farms 2. Zoos 3. Local Markets 4. Schools 5. Street Restaurants

Question 6. According to the passage, what happens to the fruits?

1. Get Spoiled 2. Get Bruised 3. Fall Off The Trees and Get Scars 4. Get Flooded 5. Price Drops

Question 7. True or False...? Because of the reason above, not getting rain at all is actually better.

1. True 2. False

Question 8. True or False...? There are technological methods that can solve droughts.

1. True 2. False

Question 9. True or False...? Waiting for rain is the only thing that can be done during droughts.

1. True 2. False

Question 10. According to the passage, what happens to the price of the fruits during the year with severe drought?

1. Skyrocket 2. Plummet 3. Gets Regulated 4. Gets Stabilized 5. Usually Remain The Same

Question 11. According to the passage, what is done to stabilize the price?

1. Making Super Plants 2. Consuming More Vegetables 3. Banning Fruit Products 4. Importing Fruits

Question 12. According to the passage, apples are...

1. Most Returned Fruit in Korea 2. Most Loved Fruit in Korea 3. Most Consumed Fruit in Korea
4. Least Favored Fruit in Korea 5. Mostly Consumed as Juice

Read the following passage carefully and answer the following questions.

한국의 인구는 계속해서 감소하고 있습니다.
[han-guk-ui in-gu-neun gye-sok-hae-seo gam-so-ha-go it-seup-ni-da.]

가장 큰 원인은 낮은 출산율입니다.
[ga-jang keun won-in-eun na-jeun chul-san-yul-ip-ni-da.]

젊은 부부들은 아기를 가지는 것을 꺼려합니다.
[jeol-meun bu-bu-deul-eun a-gi-reul ga-ji-neun geo-seul kkeo-gyreo-hap-ni-da.]

아기를 키우는 데 많은 비용이 들기 때문입니다.
[a-gi-reul ki-u-neun de man-eun bi-yong-i deul-gi ttae-mun-ip-ni-da.]

정부에서는 다양한 대책을 만들었습니다.
[jeong-bu-e-seo-neun da-yang-han dae-chaek-eul man-deul-eo-sseup-ni-da.]

아기를 갖게 되면, 지원금을 제공하기도 합니다.
[a-gi-reul gat-ge doe-myeon, ji-won-geum-eul je-gong-ha-gi-do hap-ni-da.]

반대로, 노인의 인구는 증가하고 있습니다.
[ban-dae-ro, no-in-ui in-gu-neun jeung-ga-ha-go it-seup-ni-da.]

의료기술의 발달로 인해 수명이 늘어났기 때문입니다.
[ui-ryo-gi-sul-ui bal-dal-lo in-hae su-myeong-i neul-eo-nat-gi ttae-mun-ip-ni-da.]

이러한 추세는 당분간 이어질 전망입니다.
[i-reo-han chu-se-neun dang-bun-gan i-eo-jil jeon-mang-ip-ni-da.]

노동력이 필요한 곳에서는 외국인 노동자를 필요로 합니다.
[no-dong-ryeok-i pil-yo-han go-se-seo-neun oe-guk-in no-dong-ja-reul pil-yo-ro hap-ni-da.]

농촌에서 특히 그 수요가 많습니다.
[nonh-chon-e-seo teuk-hi geu su-yo-ga man-seup-ni-da.]

미래의 한국의 모습은 지금과는 많이 다를 것 같습니다.
[mi-rae-ui han-guk-ui mo-seup-eun ji-geum-gwa-neun man-i da-reul geot gat-seup-ni-da.]

Question 1. According to the passage, what's happening to the Korean population?

1. Staying at the Same Level 2. Decreasing 3. Increasing 4. Can't Be Measured

Question 2. According to the passage, what's the biggest factor causing the above?

1. High Birth Rate 2. Low Birth Rate 3. High Mortality Rate 4. Low Mortality Rate

Question 3. True or False...? Young Korean couples are desperate to have babies.

1. True 2. False

Question 4. True or False...? The reason for the above is that it doesn't take a lot of money to raise a child.

1. True 2. False

Question 5. True or False...? The government isn't doing anything special to remedy the situation.

1. True 2. False

Question 6. According to the passage, an example of the government effort is...

1. Support Fund 2. Food Stamp 3. Free Education 4. Low Tax Rate 5. Free Baby Clothes

Question 7. What's happening to the population of elderly people?

1. Staying at the Same Level 2. Decreasing 3. Increasing 4. Can't Be Measured

Question 8. According to the passage, the reason contributing to the above trend is...

1. Advancement of Medical Technology 2. Change in Statistics 3. Better Senior Citizen Support
4. Government Funding 5. People Have More Respect Towards Senior Citizens

Question 9. According to the passage, what's expected to happen to such a trend?

1. Continue For A While 2. Will Reverse 3. Depends on the Politics 4. Can't Be Predicted

Question 10. In places where the labor force is needed, who do they need?

1. Mechanics 2. Engineers 3. Foreign Workers 4. Social Workers 5. Young People

Question 11. According to the passage, where is such demand highest?

1. Urban Area 2. Farms 3. Mountains 4. Islands 5. Factories

Question 12. True or False...? The author thinks the future of Korea will look pretty much the same as now.

1. True 2. False

Read the following passage carefully and answer the following questions.

서울의 치안은 아주 훌륭한 수준입니다.
[seo-ul-ui chi-an-eun a-ju hul-lyung-han su-jun-ip-ni-da.]

늦은 밤에도 걱정 없이 거리를 돌아다닐 수 있습니다.
[neu-jeun bam-e-do geok-jeong eop-shi geo-ril-reul dol-a-da-nil su it-seup-ni-da.]

일반인의 총기 소유는 불가능합니다.
[il-ban-in-ui chong-gi so-yu-neun bul-ga-neung-hap-ni-da.]

외국인들도 서울의 치안 수준에 대해 놀라워 합니다.
[oe-guk-in-deul-do seo-ul-ui chi-an su-jun-e dae-hae nol-la-wo hap-ni-da.]

살인사건도 거의 일어나지 않습니다.
[sal-in-sa-geon-do geo-ui il-eo-na-ji an-seup-ni-da.]

감시카메라도 곳곳에 있어, 범죄를 예방합니다
[gam-shi-ca-me-ra-do got-go-se it-sseo, beom-joe-reul ye-bang-hap-ni-da.]

하지만 조심하는 것이 가장 중요합니다
[ha-ji-man jo-shim-ha-neun geo-shi ga-jang jung-yo-hap-ni-da.]

범죄가 아주 없는 곳은 없기 때문입니다
[beom-joe-ga a-ju eop-neun go-seun eop-gi ttae-mun-ip-ni-da.]

특히 새벽 시간이 가장 위험합니다.
[teuk-hi sae-byeok shi-gan-i ga-jang wi-heom-hap-ni-da.]

사람이 많이 다니지 않기 때문입니다.
[sa-ram-i man-i da-ni-ji an-ki ttae-mun-ip-ni-da.]

어두운 곳은 피해 다녀야 합니다.
[eo-du-un go-seun pi-hae da-nyeo-ya hap-ni-da.]

그리고, 전기충격기 같은 호신용품을 갖고 다녀야 합니다.
[geu-ri-go, jeon-gi-chung-gyeok-gi ga-teun ho-shin-yong-pum-eul gat-go da-nyeo-ya hap-ni-da.]

Question 1. True or False...? According to the passage, public security in Korea is not very good.

1. True 2. False

Question 2. True or False...? According to the passage, it's impossible to walk around Seoul late in the evening.

1. True 2. False

Question 3. True or False...? Owning a gun is allowed in certain situations.

1. True 2. False

Question 4. According to the passage, foreigners feel THIS about the public security of Seoul.

1. Worried 2. Surprised 3. Terrified 4. Hopeless 5. Tired

Question 5. According to the passage, THIS happens almost never at all.

1. Robbery 2. Scam 3. Suicide 4. Homicide 5. Assault

Question 6. According to the passage, THIS is in many places to prevent crime.

1. Police Station 2. Alarms 3. Emergency Exits 4. Safety Weapons 5. Surveillance Cameras

Question 7. According to the passage, being THIS is most important.

1. Careful 2. Skeptical 3. Hopeful 4. Positive 5. Neutral

Question 8. The reason for the above is because there aren't places that don't have...

1. Death 2. Bad People 3. Accidents 4. Crime 5. Surveillance Cameras

Question 9. True or False...? It's most dangerous around dinner time.

1. True 2. False

Question 10. The reason for the above is because there aren't many...

1. Police Officers 2. Cars 3. Lights 4. People 5. Good People

Question 11. According to the passage, you have to avoid what kind of place...?

1. Bright 2. Dark 3. Dirty 4. Abandoned 5. Uncontrolled

Question 12. True or False...? Carrying around a self-defense item is not recommended because it might provoke bad guys.

1. True 2. False

Practice #48 (Difficulty ★★★★★)

Read the following passage carefully and answer the following questions.

김치의 유래에 대해서 여러가지 설이 있습니다.
[kim-chi-ui yu-rae-e dae-hae-seo yeo-reo-ga-ji seol-i it-seup-ni-da.]

삼국시대에 먹기 시작했다는 것이 가장 유력합니다.
[sam-guk-shi-dae-e meok-gi shi-jak-haet-da-neun geo-shi ga-jang yu-ryeok-hap-ni-da.]

가장 흔한 종류는 배추 김치입니다.
[ga-jang heun-han jong-ryu-neun bae-chu kim-chi-ip-ni-da.]

애초에는 김치가 하얀색이었다고 합니다.
[ae-cho-e-neun kim-chi-ga ha-yan-saek-i-eot-da-go hap-ni-da.]

고추가루를 사용하면서 빨갛게 되었습니다.
[go-chu-ga-ru-reul sa-yong-ha-myeon-seo bbal-gat-ge doe-eot-seup-ni-da.]

김치에는 굉장히 많은 유산균이 있습니다
[kim-chi-e-neun goeng-jang-hi man-eun yu-san-gyun-i it-seup-ni-da.]

발효과정을 거쳐 만들어지기 때문입니다.
[bal-hyo-gwa-jeong-eul geo-cheyo man-deul-eo-ji-gi ttae-mun-ip-ni-da.]

김치에는 조상들의 지혜가 담겨져 있습니다.
[kim-chi-e-neun jo-sang-deul-ui ji-hye-ga dam-gyeo-jyeo it-seup-ni-da.]

지역마다 다양한 종류의 김치가 있습니다.
[ji-yeok-ma-da da-yang-han jong-ryu-ui kim-chi-ga it-seup-ni-da.]

알려진 종류만 약 오십 가지가 넘습니다.
[al-lyo-jin jong-ryu-man yak o-ship ga-ji-ga neom-seup-ni-da.]

김치는 해외로도 수출이 많이 됩니다.
[kim-chi-neun hae-oe-ro-do su-chul-i man-i doep-ni-da.]

외국인들은 한국 음식하면 김치를 가장 먼저 떠올립니다.
[oe-guk-in-deul-eun han-guk eum-shik-ha-myeon kim-chi-reul ga-jang meon-jeo tteo-ol-lip-ni-da.]

Question 1. According to the passage, regarding WHAT are there many theories?

1. Origin of Kimchi 2. Origin of Korean Wrestling 3. Birth of Korean Language 4. Why Joseon Failed

Question 2. True or False...? According to the most probable theory, people started consuming it since the...

1. Stone Age 2. Bronze Age 3. Three Kingdoms Period 4. Joseon Dynasty 5. Modern Day Korea

Question 3. According to the passage, *baechu kimchi* is THIS type of kimchi.

1. Loved 2. Enjoyed 3. Common 4. Tasty 5. Hated

Question 4. According to the passage, kimchi was originally...

1. Blue 2. Green 3. White 4. Red 5. Purple

Question 5. According to the passage, what caused such change?

1. Black Pepper 2. Powdered Chili 3. Curry Powder 4. Brown Sugar 5. Pink Salt

Question 6. According to the passage, kimchi has a lot of THIS.

1. Protein 2. Lactobacillus 3. Calories 4. Fiber 5. Carbs

Question 7. The reason for the above is because kimchi goes through THIS process.

1. Fermentation 2. Fortifying 3. Deepening 4. Regulating 5. Doubling

Question 8. According to the passage, kimchi contains THIS.

1. Ancestors' Wisdom 2. Experience 3. Korean Philosophy 4. Ancient Secrets 5. Modern Technology

Question 9. According to the passage, there are various types of kimchi in different...

1. Cultures 2. Seasons 3. Regions 4. Countries 5. Houses

Question 10. True or False...? There are more than fifty types of kimchi that are still not known.

1. True 2. False

Question 11. True or False...? A lot of kimchi is exported overseas.

1. True 2. False

Question 12. True or False...? When it comes to Korean food, foreigners think of kimchi the most.

1. True 2. False

Read the following passage carefully and answer the following questions.

사람의 성격은 태어나기 전 이미 형성된다.
[sa-ram-ui seong-gyeok-eun tae-eo-na-gi jeon i-mi hyeong-seong-doen-da.]

태아들도 제각각의 특징을 갖고 있다.
[tae-a-deul-do je-gak-gak-ui teuk-jing-eul gat-go it-da.]

후천적인 요인보다 선천적인 요인이 더 큰 영향을 미친다.
[hu-cheon-jeok-in yo-in-bo-da seon-cheon-jeok-in yo-in-i deo keun yeong-hyang-eul mi-chin-da.]

후천적인 것은 학습과 경험을 통해 만들어진다.
[hu-cheon-jeok-in geo-seun hak-seup-gwa gyeong-heom-eul tong-hae man-deul-eo-jin-da.]

사회적인 능력을 기르는 것이 중요하다.
[sa-hoe-jeok-in neung-ryeok-eul gi-reu-neun geo-shi jung-yo-ha-da.]

단체 생활을 경험 하는 것이 필요하다.
[dan-che saeng-hwa-eul gyeong-heom-ha-neun geo-shi pil-yo-ha-da.]

유치원에 다니는 것을 권장한다.
[yu-chi-won-e da-ni-neun geo-seul gwon-jang-han-da.]

성격은 훈련을 통해서 교정될 수 있다.
[seong-geyok-eun hun-ryeon-eul tong-hae-seo gyo-jeong-doel su it-da.]

아주 심한 경우에는, 심리치료를 해야한다.
[a-ju shim-han gyeong-u-e-neun, shim-li-chi-ryo-reul hae-ya-han-da.]

약물 치료가 필요한 경우도 있다.
[yak-mul-chi-ryo-ga pil-yo-han gyeong-u-do it-da.]

어떤 경우에서든, 전문가의 상담을 받아야 한다.
[eo-tteon gyeong-u-e-seo-deun, jeon-mun-ga-ui sang-dam-eul ba-da-ya han-da.]

그리고, 주위 사람들의 협력이 중요하다.
[geu-ri-go, ju-wi sa-ram-deul-ui hyeop-ryeok-i jung-yo-ha-da.]

Question 1. True or False...? People's personalities are developed before they are born.

1. True 2. False

Question 2. According to the passage, even THESE have their distinct characteristics.

1. Fetuses 2. Sperms 3. Eggs 4. Animals 5. Bacteria

Question 3. True or False...? Innate factors have a bigger impact than posterior ones.

1. True 2. False

Question 4. According to the passage, posterior factors are made through...

1. Learning and Experience 2. Studying and Practicing 3. Reward 4. Trial and Error 5. Luck

Question 5. According to the passage, what does the author think is important to develop?

1. Sense of Humor 2. Survival Skills 3. Empathy 4. Social Abilities 5. Space Perception

Question 6. True or False...? The author thinks experiencing a group life is not necessary.

1. True 2. False

Question 7. True or False...? The author recommends going HERE.

1. Kindergarten 2. Church 3. Boot Camp 4. Volunteer Organization 5. Library

Question 8. According to the passage, personalities can be corrected through...

1. Learning 2. Training 3. Healing 4. Reward 5. Punishment

Question 9. According to the passage, THIS is needed if the case is serious.

1. Physical Punishment 2. Exorcism 3. Psychotherapy 4. Group Session 5. Hospitalization

Question 10. According to the passage, THIS can be needed in some cases.

1. Drug Treatment 2. Jail Time 3. Physical Punishment 4. Fine 5. Correctional Facility

Question 11. True or False...? You need counseling from an expert only if it's a danger to the society and community.

1. True 2. False

Question 12. According to the passage, what else is important?

1. Remaining Skeptical 2. Keeping an Eye for Relapse 3. Looking Out for Each Other
4. Cooperation From People Around 5. Well-Designed Rehab Plans

Read the following passage carefully and answer the following questions.

지금 과학계에서 가장 흥미로운 주제는 인공지능이다.
[ji-geum gwa-hak-gye-e-seo ga-jang heung-mi-ro-un ju-je-neun in-gong-ji-neung-i-da.]

기계가 인간처럼 생각하고 결정하는 기술을 의미한다.
[gi-gye-ga in-gan-cheo-reom saeng-gak-ha-go gyeol-jeong-ha-neun gi-sul-eul ui-mi-han-da.]

인공지능을 바라보는 시각은 엇갈린다.
[in-gong-ji-neung-eul ba-ra-bo-neun shi-gak-eun eot-gal-lin-da.]

인류에게 위협이 될 수도 있고, 희망이 될 수도 있다고 생각한다.
[in-ryu-e-ge wi-hyeop-i doel su-do it-go, hui-mang-i doel su do it-da-go saeng-gak-han-da.]

인간이 할 수 없는 위험한 일들을 대신 하는 것은 장점이다.
[in-gan-i hal su eop-neun wi-heom-han il-deul-eul dae-shin ha-neun geo-seun jang-jeom-i-da.]

인간의 일자리를 빼았는 것은 단점이다.
[in-gan-ui il-ja-ri-reul bbae-at-neun geo-seun dan-jeom-ip-da.]

하지만, 기술이 발달하면 새로운 기회가 만들어 질 것이다.
[ha-ji-man, gi-sul-i bal-dal-ha-myeon sae-ro-un gi-hoe-ga man-deul-eo jil geo-shi-da.]

급진적인 변화보다, 단계적인 변화가 권장된다.
[geup-jin-jeok-in byeon-hwa-bo-da, dan-gye-jeok-in byeon-hwa-ga gwon-jang-doen-da.]

변화로 인한 부작용을 발견하기 위해서다.
[byeon-hwa-ro in-han bu-jak-yong-eul bal-gyeon-ha-gi wi-hae-seo-da.]

기술이 발달하면, 삶의 질 또한 높아질 것이다.
[gi-sul-i bal-dal-ha-myeon, sal-mui jil tto-han nop-a-jil geo-shi-da.]

기계가 오작동을 하지 않도록, 철저히 감시해야 한다.
[gi-gye-ga o-jak-dong-eul ha-ji an-to-rok, cheol-jeo-hi gam-shi-hae-ya han-da.]

만약의 오류에 대비한, 대비책도 마련해야 한다.
[man-yak-ui o-ryu-e dae-bi-han, dae-bi-chaek-do ma-ryeon-hae-ya han-da.]

Question 1. According to the passage, what's the most interesting topic in the field of science today?

1. Time Travel 2. Space Exploration 3. Artificial Inteligence 4. Reverse Engineering 5. Hybrid Car

Question 2. According to the passage, such technology is where machines do THIS like humans.

1. Eat and Drink 2. Think and Decide 3. Assess and Measure 4. Attack and Defend 5. Read and Write

Question 3. True or False...? The views on artificial intelligence are mostly negative.

1. True 2. False

Question 4. According to the passage, it can be THESE to humankind.

1. Power and Danger 2. Asset and Liability 3. Problem and Solution 4. Threat and Hope

Question 5. According to the passage, what's an advantage of such technology?

1. Doing Dangerous Work For Humans 2. Solving Difficult Problems 3.

Question 6. According to the passage, what's the downside of such technology?

1. Making Errors 2. Taking Humans' Jobs 3. Learning Too Quickly 4. Making Rational Decisions

Question 7. True or False...? The advancement of technology will create more opportunities.

1. True 2. False

Question 8. True or False...? With the resources available, we need rational changes.

1. True 2. False

Question 9. According to the passage, the reason for the above logic is so we can find THIS due to changes.

1. Errors 2. Dangers 3. Threats 4. Side Effects 5. Warning Signs

Question 10. With the advancement of technology, what will go up?

1. Wage 2. Death Rate 3. Average Life Expectancy 4. Quality of Life 5. Crime Rate

Question 11. According to the passage, close monitoring of machines is required to prevent...

1. Rebellion 2. Malfunctions 3. Breakdown 4. Failure 5. Deaths

Question 12. According to the passage, what needs to be prepared in case of what's mentioned above?

1. Countermeasures 2. Emergency Exits 3. Laws 4. Rules and Regulations 5. Quarantine Area

Practice #41

언어를 배우는 데 있어서 가장 효과적인 방법은 모방이라고 한다.
It's said that the most effective method in learning a language is imitating.
[eon-eo-reul bae-u-neun de it-seo-seo ga-jang hyo-gwa-jeok-in bang-beop-eun mo-bang-i-ra-go han-da.]
실제로, 어린 아기들은 부모가 말하는 법을 보고 배운다.
Actually, little babies learn by watching the way their parents talk.
[shil-je-ro, eo-rin a-gi-deul-eun bu-mo-ga mal-ha-neun beop-eul bo-go bae-un-da.]
심지어, 사소한 습관까지 그대로 따라한다.
Even, they imitate their trivial habits.
[shim-ji-eo, sa-so-han seup-gwan-kka-ji geu-dae-ro tta-ra-han-da.]
몸짓과 표정을 통해 감정을 전달하는 방법도 익힌다.
They also learn the method to deliver emotions through actions and facial expressions.
[mom-jit-gwa pyo-jeong-eul tong-hae gam-jeong-eul jeon-dal-ha-neun bang-beop-do ik-hin-da.]
흥미로운 사실은, 동물들도 모방을 통해 언어를 배운다는 것이다.
The interesting fact is, animals also learn a language through imitation.
[heung-mi-ro-un sa-shil-eun, dong-mul-deul-do mo-bang-eul tong-hae eon-eo-reul bae-un-da-neun geo-shi-da.]
예를들어, 아기 강아지들은 부모가 짖는 소리를 똑같이 흉내낸다.
For example, baby puppies identically imitate the barking sound their parents make.
[ye-reul-deul-eo, a-gi gang-a-ji-deul-eun bu-mo-ga jit-neun so-ri-reul ttok-ga-chi hyung-nae-naen-da.]
언어학자들에 따르면, 태어나서 십 년 동안이 가장 중요한 시기라고 한다.
According to linguists, ten years since birth is the most important period.
[eon-eo-hak-ja-deul-e tta-reu-myeon, tae-eo-na-seo ship nyeon dong-an-i ga-jang jung-yo-han shi-gi-ra-go han-da.]
이 시기가 지나면, 새로운 언어를 배우는 것이 힘들다고 한다.
If past this period, it's said that it's difficult to learn a new language.
[i shi-gi-ga ji-na-myeon, sae-ro-un eon-eo-reul bae-u-neun geo-shi him-deul-da-go han-da.]
따라서, 어렸을때 받는 교육이 매우 중요하다.
Therefore, the education you receive while little is very important.
[tta-ra-seo, eo-reyot-sseul-ttae bat-neun gyo-yuk-i mae-u jung-yo-ha-da.]
세계에는 약 백개가 넘는 언어가 존재한다.
There are over one hundred languages in the world.
[se-gye-e-neun yak baek-gae-ga neom-neun eon-eo-ga jon-jae-han-da.]
그 중에서 가장 많은 사람들이 사용하는 언어는 중국어다.
Chinese is the language used by the largest number of people.
[geu jung-e-seo ga-jang man-eun sa-ram-deul-i sa-yong-ha-neun eon-eo-neun jung-guk-eo-da.]
기술이 발달하면, 언어를 배우는 것이 필요 없게 될 전망이다.
It's predicted that learning a new language won't be necessary if technology advances.
[gi-sul-i bal-dal-ha-myeon, eon-eo-reul bae-u-neun geo-shi pil-yo eop-ge doel jeon-mang-i-da.]

Answer Keys : (1) 4 (2) 5 (3) 1 (4) 1 (5) 2 (6) 2 (7) 2 (8) 1 (9) 2 (10) 5 (11) 1 (12) 3

Practice #42

운전을 할 때는 고도의 집중력이 필요하다.
When driving, a high level of concentration is needed.
[un-jeon-eul hal ttae-neun go-do-ui jip-jung-ryeok-i pil-yo-ha-da.]
음악을 들으면서 운전을 하는 것 도 위험하다.
It's also dangerous to drive while listening to music.
[eum-ak-eul deul-eu-myeon-seo un-jeon-eul ha-neun geot do wi-heom-ha-da.]
한국은 교통 사고 사망률이 높은 편이다.
Korea has a relatively high rate of deaths from car accidents.
[han-guk-eun gyo-tong sa-go sa-mang-ryul-i nop-eun pyeon-i-da.]
무엇보다 고령 운전자들의 사고가 많다.
Among all, there are many accidents by old drivers.
[mu-eot-bo-da go-ryeong un-jeon-ja-deul-ui sa-go-ga man-ta.]
이러한 이유에서, 팔십 세 이상의 운전은 권장되지 않는다.
For this reason, it's not recommended for those over the age of eighty to drive.
[i-reo-han i-yu-e-seo, pal-ship se i-sang-ui un-jeon-eun gwon-jang-doe-ji an-neun-da.]
그대신, 그들은 무료로 대중교통을 사용할 수 있다.
Instead, they can use public transportation for free.
[geu-dae-shin, geu-deul-eun mu-ryo-ro dae-jung-gyo-tong-eul sa-yong-hal su it-da.]
미래에는, 사람이 직접 운전하지 않아도 되는 시대가 올 것이다.
In the future, there will be a time where people don't have to drive.
[mi-rae-e-neun, sa-ram-i jik-jeop un-jeon-ha-ji an-a-do doe-neun shi-dae-ga ol geo-shi-da.]
과학자들이 열심히 연구하고 있지만, 아직 완벽하지 않다.
Scientists are researching it zealously, it's not perfect yet.
[gwa-hak-ja-deul-i yeol-shim-hi yeon-gu-ha-go it-ji-man, a-jik wan-byeok-ha-ji an-ta.]
앞으로 많은 시행착오를 겪어야 할 것이다.
For some time ahead, they will have to go through a lot of trial and error.
[ap-eu-ro man-eun shi-haeng-chak-o-reul gyeok-eo-ya hal geo-shi-da.]
그리고, 자동차를 소유하는 것이 필요 없게 될 것이다.
And, it won't be necessary to own a car.
[geu-ri-go, ja-dong-cha-reul so-yu-ha-neun geo-shi pil-yo eop-ge doel geo-shi-da.]
하늘을 나는 자동차도 등장 할 것이다.
Flying cars will make an appearance.
[ha-neul-eul na-neun ja-dong-cha-do deung-jang hal geo-shi-da.]

이 모든 것은 공상과학 영화 속의 이야기가 아니다.
All these are not a story from a sci-fi movie.
[i mo-deun geo-seun gong-sang-gwa-hak yeong-hwa sok-ui
-ya-gi-ga a-ni-da.]

Answer Keys : (1) 1 (2) 4 (3) 2 (4) 5 (5) 2 (6) 4 (7) 1 (8) 2
(9) 2 (10) 1 (11) 1 (12) 2

Practice #43

한국은 지금 남과 북으로 나뉘어져 있습니다.
Korea is currently divided into north and south.
[han-guk-eun ji-geum nam-gwa buk-eu-ro na-nwi-eo-jyeo it-
seup-ni-da]
반 세기 전 있었던 전쟁 때문입니다.
It's because of a war that took place a half-century ago.
[ban se-gi jeon it-seot-deon jeon-jaeng ttae-mun-ip-ni-da.]
같은 민족이지만, 다른 이념으로 인해 싸웠습니다.
Although they are of the same ethnic race, they fought because
of different ideologies.
[ga-teun min-jok-i-ji-man, da-reum i-nyeom-eu-ro in-hae ssa-
wot-seup-ni-da.]
대부분의 사람들은 고향을 떠났습니다.
Most of the people left their hometowns.
[dae-bu-bun-ui sa-ram-deul-eun go-hyang-eul tteo-nat-seup-ni-
da.]
그리고, 가족들과 헤어져야 했습니다.
And, they had to part from their family.
[geu-ri-go, ga-jok-deul-gwa he-eo-jyeo-ya haet-seup-ni-da.]
정치인들은 문제를 해결하기 위해 노력하고 있습니다.
Politicians are putting in efforts to solve the problem.
[jeong-chi-in-deul-eun mun-je-reul hae-gyeol-ha-gi wi-hae no-
ryeok-ha-go it-seup-ni-da.]
하지만 통일이 되려면 시간이 많이 필요합니다.
But in order for unification to happen, it requires a lot of time.
[ha-ji-man tong-il-i doe-ryeo-myeon shi-gan-i man-i pil-yo-hap-
ni-da.]
다행히도, 남과 북은 같은 언어를 사용합니다.
Luckily, north and south use the same language.
[da-haeng-hi-do, nam-gwa buk-eun ga-teun eon-eo-reul sa-
yong-hap-ni-da.]
하지만 문화는 많이 차이가 납니다.
But cultures are quite different.
[ha-ji-man mun-hwa-neun man-i cha-i-ga nap-ni-da.]
경제력도 큰 격차가 생겼습니다.
A large gap between their economic powers has been made, too.
[mo-deun sa-go-neun ye-bang-hal su it-seup-ni-da.]
만약 남과 북이 합쳐지면, 단점보다는 장점이 많아질 것
입니다.
If the south and north get unified, there will be more pros than
cons.
[man-yak-eul dae-bi-hae, jip-e so-hwa-gi-reul sa no-a-ya hap-
ni-da.]
여행 갈 수 있는 곳도 더욱 많아지겠죠.
There will be more places to travel, too.
[geu-ri-go, bi-sang-gu-ga eo-di it-neun-ji gi-eok-hae-ya hap-ni-
da.]

Answer Keys : (1) 2 (2) 2 (3) 4 (4) 2 (5) 2 (6) 2 (7) 2 (8) 2

(9) 5 (10) 2 (11) 2 (12) 3

Practice #44

감기에 걸리는 이유는 우리가 생각하는 것 보다 많습니다.
There are more reasons than we think as to why we catch a
cold.
[gam-gi-e geol-li-neun i-yu-neun u-ri-ga saeng-gak-ha-neun
geot bo-da man-seup-ni-da.]
그리고, 상식과 다른 것도 많습니다.
And, there is a lot that is different from common sense.
[geu-ri-go, sang-sik-gwa da-reun geot-do man-seup-ni-da.]
예를들어, 우리는 추운 곳에서 감기가 더 잘 걸린다고 생
각합니다.
For example, we think we are more likely to catch a cold in
cold places.
[ye-reul-deul-eo, u-ri-neun chu-un go-se-seo gam-gi-ga deo jal
geol-lin-da-go saeng-gak-hap-ni-da.]
하지만 오히려 추운 곳에서는 감기 균이 활동하지 못한다
고 합니다.
But it's said that rather in cold places, cold viruses can't be
active.
[ha-ji-man o-hi-yreo chu-un go-se-seo-neun gam-gi gyun-i
hwal-dong-ha-ji mot-han-da-go hap-ni-da.]
기온의 차이가 크게 날 때 감기에 더 잘 걸립니다.
We catch a cold more easily when the temperature difference is
big.
[gi-on-ui cha-i-ga keu-ge nal ttae gam-gi-e deo jal geol-lip-ni-
da.]
우리 몸의 면역체계가 변화에 대처하지 못하기 때문입니
다.
It's because our immune system can't cope with changes.
[u-ri mom-ui myeon-yeok-che-gye-ga byeon-hwa-e dae-cheo-
ha-ji mot-ha-gi ttae-mun-ip-ni-da.]
그래서, 항상 여분의 옷을 가지고 다니는 것이 권장됩니
다.
So, it's recommended to always carry extra clothes.
[geu-rae-seo, hang-sang yeo-bun-ui o-seul ga-ji-go da-ni-neun
geo-shi gwon-jang-doep-ni-da.]
감기에 걸리면, 목을 따뜻하게 하는 것이 효과적입니다.
When you catch a cold, it's effective to keep your neck warm.
[gam-gi-e geol-li-myeon, mok-eul tta-tteut-ha-ge ha-neun geo-
shi hyo-gwa-jeok-ip-ni-da.]
목도리를 하는 것이 가장 쉬운 방법입니다.
Putting on a scar is the easiest method.
[mok-do-ri-reul ha-neun geo-shi ga-jang shwi-un bang-beop-ip-
ni-da.]
술을 마시는 것은 피해야 합니다.
Drinking should be avoided.
[sul-eul ma-shi-neun geo-seun pi-hae-ya hap-ni-da.]
탈수로 인해 몸의 저항력이 떨어지기 때문입니다.
Because of dehydration, the body's resistance drops down.
[tal-su-ro in-hae mom-ui jeo-hang-ryeok-i tteol-eo-ji-gi ttae-
mun-ip-ni-da.]
하지만 따뜻한 포도주를 마시는 것이 전통인 나라도 있습
니다.
But there are countries where drinking warm wine is a tradition.
[ha-ji-man tta-tteut-han po-do-ju-reul ma-shi-neun geo-shi jeon-
tong-in na-ra-do it-seup-ni-da.]

Answer Keys : (1) 1 (2) 3 (3) 3 (4) 1 (5) 2 (6) 2 (7) 1 (8) 3
(9) 4 (10) 4 (11) 3 (12) 3

Practice #45

한반도는 자연재해가 많지 않은 편입니다.
Korean peninsula doesn't have a lot of natural disasters.
[han-ban-do-neun ja-yeon-jae-hae-ga man-chi an-eun
pyeon-ip-ni-da.]
하지만 태풍은 아주 파괴력이 큽니다.
But hurricanes are very destructive.
[ha-ji-man tae-pung-eun a-ju pa-goe-ryeok-i keup-ni-da.]
태풍이 오면 엄청난 양의 비가 내리고, 강한 바람이 붑
니다.
When a hurricane comes, a tremendous amount of rain
pours, and the wind blows strongly.
[tae-pung-i o-myeon eom-cheong-nan yang-ui bi-ga nae-ri-
go, gang-han ba-ram-i bup-ni-da.]
차량의 운행이 금지 될 정도입니다.
To the degree where driving a car is even prohibited.
[cha-ryang-ui un-haeng-i geum-ji doel jeong-do-ip-ni-da.]
하지만 가장 큰 피해를 보는 곳은 농촌입니다.
But the places where it gets the most damage are farms.
[ha-ji-man ga-jang keun pi-hae-reul bo-neun go-seun nong-
chon-ip-ni-da.]
과일이 나무에서 떨어지고, 상처가 납니다.
Fruits fall from trees and get scarred.
[gwa-il-i na-mu-e-seo tteol-eo-ji-go, sang-cheo-ga nap-ni-
da.]
반대로, 비가 너무 오지 않아서 문제가 되기도 합니다.
Conversely, it sometimes becomes troublesome by not
raining at all.
[ban-dae-ro, bi-ga neo-mu o-ji an-a-seo mun-je-ga doe-gi-
do hap-ni-da.]
가뭄이 찾아오면, 사람이 할 수 있는 것은 별로 없습니
다.
When a drought hits, there aren't many things a human can
do.
[ga-mum-i cha-ja-o-myeon, sa-ram-i hal su it-neun geo-seun
byeol-lo eop-seup-ni-da.]
비가 오기만을 기다릴 수 밖에 없습니다.
We just need to wait for it to rain.
[bi-ga o-gi-man-eul gi-da-ril su bak-e eop-seup-ni-da.]
가뭄이 심한 해에는, 과일 값이 폭등합니다.
In a year with a severe drought, fruit prices skyrocket.
[ga-mum-i shim-han ttae-e-neun gwa-il gap-shi pok-deung-
hap-ni-da.]
그래서 과일을 수입해서 가격을 안정시키기도 합니다.
So the price is sometimes stabilized by importing fruits.
[geu-rae-seo gwa-il-eul su-ip-hae-seo ga-gyeok-eul an-
jeong-shi-ki-gi-do hap-ni-da.]
한국에서 가장 많이 소비되는 과일은 사과입니다.
The most consumed fruit in Korea is the apple.
[han-gul-e-seo ga-jang man-i so-bi-doe-neun gwa-il-eun
sa-gwa-ip-ni-da.]

Answer Keys : (1) 3 (2) 2 (3) 4 (4) 1 (5) 1 (6) 3 (7) 2 (8) 2
(9) 1 (10) 1 (11) 4 (12) 3

Practice #46

한국의 인구는 계속해서 감소하고 있습니다.
The population in Korea continues to decline.
[han-guk-ui in-gu-neun gye-sok-hae-seo gam-so-ha-go it-seup-ni-
da.]
가장 큰 원인은 낮은 출산율입니다.
The biggest factor is the low birth rate.
[ga-jang keun won-in-eun na-jeun chul-san-yul-ip-ni-da.]
젊은 부부들은 아기를 가지는 것을 꺼려합니다.
Young couples are hesitant to have a child.
[jeol-meun bu-bu-deul-eun a-gi-reul ga-ji-neun geo-seul kkeo-
gyeo-hap-ni-da.]
아기를 키우는 데 많은 비용이 들기 때문입니다.
Because it costs a lot to raise a child.
[a-gi-reul ki-u-neun de man-eun bi-yong-i deul-gi ttae-mun-ip-ni-
da.]
정부에서는 다양한 대책을 만들었습니다.
The government made various countermeasures.
[jeong-bu-e-seo-neun da-yang-han dae-chaek-eul man-deul-eo-
sseup-ni-da.]
아기를 갖게 되면, 지원금을 제공하기도 합니다.
If you have a baby, you are sometimes provided support money.
[a-gi-reul gat-ge doe-myeon, ji-won-geum-eul je-gong-ha-gi-do
hap-ni-da.]
반대로, 노인의 인구는 증가하고 있습니다.
Conversely, the population of old people is increasing.
[ban-dae-ro, no-in-ui in-gu-neun jeung-ga-ha-go it-seup-ni-da.]
의료기술의 발달로 인해 수명이 늘어났기 때문입니다.
It's because the lifespan has been extended due to the advancement
of medical technology.
[ui-ryo-gi-sul-ui bal-dal-lo in-hae su-myeong-i neul-eo-nat-gi ttae-
mun-ip-ni-da.]
이러한 추세는 당분간 이어질 전망입니다.
This kind of trend is expected to continue for a while.
[i-reo-han chu-se-neun dang-bun-gan i-eo-jil jeon-mang-ip-ni-da.]
노동력이 필요한 곳에서는 외국인 노동자를 필요로 합니다.
When there is a labor force needed, foreign workers are required.
[no-dong-ryeok-i pil-yo-han go-se-seo-neun oe-guk-in no-dong-ja-
reul pil-yo-ro hap-ni-da.]
농촌에서 특히 그 수요가 많습니다.
Such demand is especially high in farms.
[nonh-chon-e-seo teuk-hi geu su-yo-ga man-seup-ni-da.]
미래의 한국의 모습은 지금과는 많이 다를 것 같습니다.
I think the future of Korea will be quite different from the present.
[mi-rae-ui han-guk-ui mo-seup-eun ji-geum-gwa-neun man-i da-
reul geot gat-seup-ni-da.]

Answer Keys : (1) 2 (2) 2 (3) 2 (4) 2 (5) 2 (6) 1 (7) 3 (8) 1
(9) 1 (10) 3 (11) 2 (12) 2

Practice #47

서울의 치안은 아주 훌륭한 수준입니다.
The security in Seoul is at a very high level.
[seo-ul-ui chi-an-eun a-ju hul-lyung-han su-jun-ip-ni-da.]
늦은 밤에도 걱정 없이 거리를 돌아다닐 수 있습니다.
You can walk around the streets at late night without having to worry.
[neu-jeun bam-e-do geok-jeong eop-shi geo-ril-reul dol-a-da-nil su it-seup-ni-da.]
일반인의 총기 소유는 불가능합니다.
It's impossible for general people to own guns.
[il-ban-in-ui chong-gi so-yu-neun bul-ga-neung-hap-ni-da.]
외국인들도 서울의 치안 수준에 대해 놀라워 합니다.
Foreigners are surprised by the level of security in Seoul, too.
[oe-guk-in-deul-do seo-ul-ui chi-an su-jun-e dae-hae nol-la-wo hap-ni-da.]
살인사건도 거의 일어나지 않습니다.
Homicides rarely happen too.
[sal-in-sa-geon-do geo-ui il-eo-na-ji an-seup-ni-da.]
감시카메라도 곳곳에 있어, 범죄를 예방합니다.
There are also surveillance cameras all over the place, preventing crimes.
[gam-shi-ca-me-ra-do got-go-se it-sseo, beom-joe-reul ye-bang-hap-ni-da.]
하지만 조심하는 것이 가장 중요합니다.
But being careful is most important.
[ha-ji-man jo-shim-ha-neun geo-shi ga-jang jung-yo-hap-ni-da.]
범죄가 아주 없는 곳은 없기 때문입니다.
There aren't places where there's completely no crime.
[beom-joe-ga a-ju eop-neun go-seun eop-gi ttae-mun-ip-ni-da.]
특히 새벽 시간이 가장 위험합니다.
The early hours of the morning are especially important.
[teuk-hi sae-byeok shi-gan-i ga-jang wi-heom-hap-ni-da.]
사람이 많이 다니지 않기 때문입니다.
It's because there aren't many people walking around.
[sa-ram-i man-i da-ni-ji an-ki ttae-mun-ip-ni-da.]
어두운 곳은 피해 다녀야 합니다.
You need to avoid dark places.
[eo-du-un go-seun pi-hae da-nyeo-ya hap-ni-da.]
그리고, 전기충격기 같은 호신용품을 갖고 다녀야 합니다.
And, you need to carry self-defense items such as a stun gun.
[geu-ri-go, jeon-gi-chung-gyeok-gi ga-teun ho-shin-yong-pum-eul gat-go da-nyeo-ya hap-ni-da.]

Answer Keys : (1) 2 (2) 2 (3) 2 (4) 2 (5) 4 (6) 5 (7) 1 (8) 4 (9) 2 (10) 4 (11) 2 (12) 2

Practice #48

김치의 유래에 대해서 여러가지 설이 있습니다.
There are many theories regarding the origin of kimchi.
[kim-chi-ui yu-rae-e dae-hae-seo yeo-reo-ga-ji seol-i it-seup-ni-da.]
삼국시대에 먹기 시작했다는 것이 가장 유력합니다.
But the most convincing one is that it started being eaten around the Three Kingdoms Period.
[sam-guk-shi-dae-e meok-gi shi-jak-haet-da-neun geo-shi ga-jang yu-ryeok-hap-ni-da.]
가장 흔한 종류는 배추 김치입니다.
The most common type is baechu kimchi.
[ga-jang heun-han jong-ryu-neun bae-chu kim-chi-ip-ni-da.]
애초에는 김치가 하얀색이었다고 합니다.
In the beginning, it's said that kimchi was white.
[ae-cho-e-neun kim-chi-ga ha-yan-saek-i-eot-da-go hap-ni-da.]
고추가루를 사용하면서 빨갛게 되었습니다.
It became red with the start of the use of powdered chili.
[go-chu-ga-ru-reul sa-yong-ha-myeon-seo bbal-gat-ge doe-eot-seup-ni-da.]
김치에는 굉장히 많은 유산균이 있습니다.
There is a lot of lactobacillus in kimchi.
[kim-chi-e-neun goeng-jang-hi man-eun yu-san-gyun-i it-seup-ni-da.]
발효과정을 거쳐 만들어지기 때문입니다.
It's because it's made through the fermentation process.
[bal-hyo-gwa-jeong-eul geo-cheyo man-deul-eo-ji-gi ttae-mun-ip-ni-da.]
김치에는 조상들의 지혜가 담겨져 있습니다.
Kimchi contains the wisdom of ancestors.
[kim-chi-e-neun jo-sang-deul-ui ji-hye-ga dam-gyeo-jyeo it-seup-ni-da.]
지역마다 다양한 종류의 김치가 있습니다.
By region, there are various types of kimchi.
[ji-yeok-ma-da da-yang-han jong-ryu-ui kim-chi-ga it-seup-ni-da.]
알려진 종류만 약 오십 가지가 넘습니다.
Just counting the known types, there are over 50.
[al-lyo-jin jong-ryu-man yak o-ship ga-ji-ga neom-seup-ni-da.]
김치는 해외로도 수출이 많이 됩니다.
Kimchi is exported overseas a lot.
[kim-chi-neun hae-oe-ro-do su-chul-i man-i doep-ni-da.]
외국인들은 한국 음식하면 김치를 가장 먼저 떠올립니다.
Foreigners think of kimchi first when it comes to Korean food.
[oe-guk-in-deul-eun han-guk eum-shik-ha-myeon kim-chi-reul ga-jang meon-jeo tteo-ol-lip-ni-da.]

Answer Keys : (1) 1 (2) 3 (3) 3 (4) 3 (5) 2 (6) 2 (7) 1 (8) 1 (9) 3 (10) 2 (11) 1 (12) 1

Practice #49

사람의 성격은 태어나기 전 이미 형성된다.
A person's personality is developed even before birth.
[sa-ram-ui seong-gyeok-eun tae-eo-na-gi jeon i-mi hyeong-seong-doen-da.]
태아들도 제각각의 특징을 갖고 있다.
Even fetuses have their uniqueness.
[tae-a-deul-do je-gak-gak-ui teuk-jing-eul gat-go it-da.]
후천적인 요인보다 선천적인 요인이 더 큰 영향을 미친다.
Innate causes make a greater impact than acquired causes.
[hu-cheon-jeok-in yo-in-bo-da seon-cheon-jeok-in yo-in-i deo keun yeong-hyang-eul mi-chin-da.]
후천적인 것은 학습과 경험을 통해 만들어진다.
Acquired causes are made through learning and experience.
[hu-cheon-jeok-in geo-seun hak-seup-gwa gyeong-heom-eul tong-hae man-deul-eo-jin-da.]
사회적인 능력을 기르는 것이 중요하다.
It's important to develop social skills.
[sa-hoe-jeok-in neung-ryeok-eul gi-reu-neun geo-shi jung-yo-ha-da.]
단체 생활을 경험 하는 것이 필요하다.
It's necessary to experience a group life.
[dan-che saeng-hwa-eul gyeong-heom-ha-neun geo-shi pil-yo-ha-da.]
유치원에 다니는 것을 권장한다.
It's recommended to go to the kindergarten.
[yu-chi-won-e da-ni-neun geo-seul gwon-jang-han-da.]
성격은 훈련을 통해서 교정될 수 있다.
Personality can be fixed through training.
[seong-geyok-eun hun-ryeon-eul tong-hae-seo gyo-jeong-doel su it-da.]
아주 심한 경우에는, 심리치료를 해야한다.
In severe cases, psychotherapy needs to be done.
[a-ju shim-han gyeong-u-e-neun, shim-li-chi-ryo-reul hae-ya-han-da.]
약물 치료가 필요한 경우도 있다.
There are cases where drug treatment is necessary.
[yak-mul-chi-ryo-ga pil-yo-han gyeong-u-do it-da.]
어떤 경우에서든, 전문가의 상담을 받아야 한다.
In any case, you need to get a consultation from an expert.
[eo-tteon gyeong-u-e-seo-deun, jeon-mun-ga-ui sang-dam-eul ba-da-ya han-da.]
그리고, 주위 사람들의 협력이 중요하다.
And, cooperation from people around you is important.
[geu-ri-go, ju-wi sa-ram-deul-ui hyeop-ryeok-i jung-yo-ha-da.]

Answer Keys : (1) 1 (2) 1 (3) 1 (4) 1 (5) 4 (6) 2 (7) 1 (8) 2
(9) 3 (10) 1 (11) 2 (12) 4

Practice #50

지금 과학계에서 가장 흥미로운 주제는 인공지능이다.
The most interesting subject in the field of science is artificial intelligence.
[ji-geum gwa-hak-gye-e-seo ga-jang heung-mi-ro-un ju-je-neun in-gong-ji-neung-i-da.]
기계가 인간처럼 생각하고 결정하는 기술을 의미한다.
It means a machine thinking and deciding like a human.
[gi-gye-ga in-gan-cheo-reom saeng-gak-ha-go gyeol-jeong-ha-neun gi-sul-eul ui-mi-han-da.]
인공지능을 바라보는 시각은 엇갈린다.
There are mixed opinions regarding artificial intelligence.
[in-gong-ji-neung-eul ba-ra-bo-neun shi-gak-eun eot-gal-lin-da.]
인류에게 위협이 될 수도 있고, 희망이 될 수도 있다고 생각한다.
(People) think that it could be a threat to humans, and also hope.
[in-ryu-e-ge wi-hyeop-i doel su-do it-go, hui-mang-i doel su do it-da-go saeng-gak-han-da.]
인간이 할 수 없는 위험한 일들을 대신 하는 것은 장점이다.
Being able to do the dangerous things humans can't do is an advantage.
[in-gan-i hal su eop-neun wi-heom-han il-deul-eul dae-shin ha-neun geo-seun jang-jeom-i-da.]
인간의 일자리를 빼앗는 것은 단점이다.
Taking away human's jobs is a drawback.
[in-gan-ui il-ja-ri-reul bbae-at-neun geo-seun dan-jeom-ip-da.]
하지만, 기술이 발달하면 새로운 기회가 만들어 질 것이다.
But, there will be new opportunities made when technology advances.
[ha-ji-man, gi-sul-i bal-dal-ha-myeon sae-ro-un gi-hoe-ga man-deul-eo jil geo-shi-da.]
급진적인 변화보다, 단계적인 변화가 권장된다.
Rather than radical changes, gradual changes are recommended.
[geup-jin-jeok-in byeon-hwa-bo-da, dan-gye-jeok-in byeon-hwa-ga gwon-jang-doen-da.]
변화로 인한 부작용을 발견하기 위해서다.
It's to discover the side effects caused by changes.
[byeon-hwa-ro in-han bu-jak-yong-eul bal-gyeon-ha-gi wi-hae-seo-da.]
기술이 발달하면, 삶의 질 또한 높아질 것이다.
If technology advances, the quality of life will also increase.
[gi-sul-i bal-dal-ha-myeon, sal-mui jil tto-han nop-a-jil geo-shi-da.]
기계가 오작동을 하지 않도록, 철저히 감시해야 한다.
To keep the machines from malfunctioning, you need to monitor (them) closely.
[gi-gye-ga o-jak-dong-eul ha-ji an-to-rok, cheol-jeo-hi gam-shi-hae-ya han-da.]
만약의 오류에 대비한, 대비책도 마련해야 한다.
Countermeasures must be prepared, in case of an error.
[man-yak-ui o-ryu-e dae-bi-han, dae-bi-chaek-do ma-ryeon-hae-ya han-da.]

Answer Keys : (1) 3 (2) 2 (3) 2 (4) 4 (5) 1 (6) 2 (7) 1 (8) 2
(9) 4 (10) 4 (11) 2 (12) 1